D1420977

HOME BAKING

CAKES
& BAKES

HOME BAKING

CAKES
& BAKES

Wendy Hobson

AURA

This edition published in 2013
by Baker & Taylor (UK) Limited,
Bicester, Oxfordshire

Copyright © 2013 Arcturus Publishing Limited
26/27 Bickels Yard, 151–153 Bermondsey Street
London SE1 3HA

ISBN: 978-1-90940-941-5
AD002700EN

Printed in China

Contents

✱✱✱✱✱✱✱✱

Introduction

❋❋❋❋❋❋❋❋

There is something wonderfully satisfying about baking your own cakes; taking one out of a box or unwrapping it from cellophane is just not the same. Perhaps it is the sheer perfection of most shop-bought cakes that is off-putting. We prefer those slight idiosyncrasies and imperfections that reveal the effort and care that have gone into our own sweet treats, made especially to share with family and friends.

This collection is designed to give you more than a hundred traditional cake and bake recipes, from simple cupcakes to fruit cakes and teabreads. There are delightfully old-fashioned British cakes and international favourites too, so you can try your hand at everything from a Classic Victoria Sponge to a Tunisian Orange Cake. That means there's a great range of flavours and styles, so everyone should find plenty of options to suit their tastes and the particular occasion. There's even a section for those who have to follow a gluten-free diet.

Whether you are baking for a birthday party, afternoon tea, a church cake sale, a gift for your grandmother or just sheer self-indulgence, you are sure to enjoy working your way through the options.

INGREDIENTS

All the ingredients will be readily available in your local supermarket, so whichever cake you decide to bake you won't have to go hunting for obscure ingredients – you should find everything you need in the baking section.

That's another good thing about home baking, of course – you know exactly what has gone into your cake, whereas with a shop-bought one you may feel the need to read the small print on the label to find out what preservatives and other ingredients it contains. This is particularly advantageous if you have any food allergies or intolerances.

METHODS

Most traditional cakes are not difficult to make. In the following pages you'll find instructions on the main techniques used throughout the book, with detailed explanations as to why the cake is made in that way. This will be useful for beginners who are starting from scratch as well as for those who have been baking for some time but want to learn more about the fundamental techniques.

However, you may prefer to go straight to the recipes and start baking – and that's fine, because all the recipes give you step-by-step instructions so you know exactly what you are meant to do and what you can expect the results to be.

EVERYDAY CAKES

There are plenty of cakes in the book that use the all-in-one method. This is great for simple tea-time offerings, or when someone rings and asks if they can pop in to see you in an hour. How impressive to be able to offer them a slice of homemade cake, still slightly warm from the oven. They will really know you are pleased to see them.

For those people with families, simple cakes are great fun to make with the children – and they're ideal to take to the school bake sale.

SPECIAL GIFTS

You can bake cakes of all kinds to give as gifts to family and friends. The fact that you have taken the time and trouble to make something especially for them will be much appreciated, and presenting your hosts at a party with a homemade cake makes a pleasing change from a bottle of wine or some flowers. One tip, though, if you are making a cake for a special occasion: it's best to have a practice run at a new recipe.

MAKING YOUR CAKES YOUR OWN

Always remember that a recipe is only a guide; experiment with different ingredients and see how they alter the flavours and textures. Make a note of particular successes and also the experiments that didn't work so well so that you know what to repeat or to revisit with amendments – and above all, enjoy your baking!

CHAPTER 1

****

GETTING STARTED

Given the array of delicious cakes and bakes in this little book, you might think that you need a lot of fancy equipment in your kitchen. You may be concerned that you have a lot to learn about baking techniques, too. Not so! As long as you have a few kitchen basics and one or two cake tins, there's nothing to stop you creating some delicious cakes and bakes for your friends and family.

Equipment

✳ ✳ ✳ ✳ ✳ ✳ ✳ ✳

*This book is not about making delicate and complex patisserie –
it is about traditional cakes and bakes, so you probably
already have everything you need in the kitchen.*

It's certainly not worth dashing out to specialist kitchen shops to stock up on obscure gadgets. If you do, you can be sure that most of them will stay in the cupboard taking up space. If you start with the basics, you will soon work out for yourself whether you need any extras.

MEASURING

Measuring accurately is an important first step to success.

Kitchen scales Choose scales that are accurate, easy to clean and calibrated to show metric or imperial measurements; most are now electronic, so you can change the settings at the touch of a button.

Measuring jugs A Pyrex measuring jug is very useful as it can also be used for heating in the microwave. Some measuring jugs have the calibration on the inside so you can see more easily as you pour in the liquid – look out for them as they are very convenient.

VALUE AND QUALITY

If you discover a passion for baking, it's better to buy a few good-quality items and add to your equipment gradually. In the long run, they will be better value and you'll get better results than you will from cheap cookware and accessories.

Measuring spoons A set of measuring spoons will give far more reliable results than your cutlery. When measuring 1 tsp or 1 tbsp, fill the spoon then flatten the top with a knife to get the correct measure.

Cup measures You may have recipe books – or find recipes on the internet – in which the ingredients are given in cups. These are based on volume, not weight. The easiest way to use these recipes is to buy a set of cup measures. For liquid, 1 cup = 250ml/8fl oz. For other ingredients, fill the cup and level the top. Cup measures are based on volume, so if you were to weigh the ingredients, you would find that 1 cup of flour weighs about 100g/4oz, whereas 1 cup of sugar weighs around 225g/8oz, for example. Rather than try to remember or look up conversions, if you wish to use recipes with cup measurements you will save yourself a lot of time and confusion by just purchasing the right inexpensive equipment at the outset.

MIXING

All you really need for mixing your cake batter is a couple of bowls and spoons.

Bowls A large mixing bowl is a must. A Pyrex one is useful as you can see if you have mixed all the ingredients thoroughly, but my own favourite is a melamine bowl with a handle on one side and a lip on the other – it looks like a cross between a giant's teacup and a jug. It's easier to hold, lighter, and more convenient when transferring ingredients into a cake tin.

A few smaller bowls are also useful for mixing separate ingredients – glass pudding basins come in handy sizes. When whisking, you need a wide bowl that allows you to whisk the air into the mix.

Spoons and things A couple of wooden spoons are good for mixing, plus large metal spoons for folding. A little hand whisk is useful, as is a flexible scraper for getting the last of the mixture out of the bowl.

Mixers and processors The most useful tool of all is a little electric hand whisk; the beaters are easy to wash, it can be used for beating and whisking, and it doesn't take much space in the cupboard. Plus, of course, it replaces a lot of elbow grease. You can also use your food processor, especially for all-in-one mixes and for chopping.

BAKING

Here are your few essentials for the baking part of cake-making.

Baking tins The following tins will see you a long way: a 20cm/8in square, a 20cm/8in round springform (which means the bottom is separate and the sides clip tight), a 12-hole cupcake tin, a 12-hole muffin tin and a 900g/2lb loaf tin, all of them non-stick. Sandwich tins, which are shallow cake tins, are also useful. Before equipping yourself fully you may like to try flexible silicone cookware and see which you prefer.

Lining papers If you have reliable silicone cookware, you shouldn't need to line your 'tins'. However, it's worth going to the trouble of lining most other cake tins so that your cakes turn out easily without sticking. Don't use ordinary greaseproof paper – line them with baking paper (or 'parchment'), which has a silicone layer. You can buy it on a roll to cut to shape, or as ready-cut circles for the base of cake tins, or strips for the sides. Shaped cupcake, muffin, cake tin and loaf tin liners are also available; they will save you time but cost a little more. See page 18 for information on how to line your tins.

You can also obtain reusable silicone sheets or circles with which to line your tins. Have a look in the stores and experiment to see which you prefer. Silicone baking sheet liners are also very useful indeed.

Cooling rack This is not an essential – you can use a grill rack instead. A rack helps a cake to cool quickly as the air can circulate on all sides.

Ingredients

✳ ✳ ✳ ✳ ✳ ✳ ✳ ✳

If you don't need fancy equipment, you certainly don't need fancy ingredients to enjoy baking delicious cakes – everything will be found in your local supermarket.

The staples of baking are flour, butter, sugar and eggs – and you can't get much simpler than that! Fortunately for us, however, even those staples come in all kinds of varieties that we can mix and match to create new and interesting cakes.

FLOURS
Most of the cakes are made with plain flour, with the addition of baking powder to help it rise; you can substitute self-raising flour if you prefer. Wholemeal flours are slightly heavier, so they are generally used for cakes that are more robust in style. Mixing half plain and half wholemeal flour gives good results.

For gluten-free cakes, you will need a gluten-free flour mix, or you can use rice flour or gram flour, for example. These will be found in the gluten-free or international sections of your supermarket or in Asian stores. Ground nuts are also used in some of the recipes instead of wheat flours.

Raising agents include baking powder, bicarbonate of soda and cream of tartar. Again, there are gluten-free versions.

FATS AND OILS
Butter is listed in many of the recipes but you can use a spread instead, as long as it is suitable for baking – check the label. I use unsalted butter.

Cakes made with oil instead of butter look slightly strange at first when you are mixing

them – the batter is more runny and has a slightly greasy-looking texture – but the results are moist and light.

SWEET THINGS

Sugar comes in many variations, of course: caster, golden caster, granulated, dark and light soft brown, crunchy demerara, super-fine icing. If you are in doubt, caster sugar is most often used for cakes as it is a fine sugar.

You can also sweeten cakes with honey, syrup, treacle or agave syrup – all will give a slightly different flavour. I also use canned caramel – you'll find it in the supermarket with the condensed milk. Sweet fruits will also flavour your cakes.

EGGS

The recipes generally use medium eggs. If you have small or large eggs, remember that you may need to add a little more liquid, usually milk, or a little more flour to make sure the mixture is the right consistency.

OTHER INGREDIENTS

And then there are all those lovely fresh and dried fruits and vegetables that can bring texture, colour and flavour – not to mention valuable nutrients to make our indulgence a little more healthy. The range of spices on offer also gives us the opportunity to make cakes that bring us the flavours of the Caribbean or the Far East.

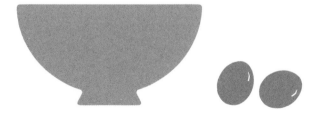

Basic Methods

All the recipes give you step-by-step instructions, but if you are new to baking, here's a little introduction to baking technique, plus more detail on some basic methods.

FOR BEGINNERS

Here are a few guidelines for beginners so you start off on the right foot. If you have baked a few cakes in your time, you might want to skip over this section.

Preparation Make sure your kitchen surfaces are clean; basic kitchen hygiene applies however fancy the cake. An apron is a good idea, too.

Read through the recipe so that it doesn't hold any surprises. Gather the ingredients in a convenient spot, making sure you still have enough working room, especially if you are rolling out something on the worktop. Get your cake tins out, too, with any utensils and baking paper you are going to need.

Next turn on the oven to the recommended temperature so it can heat up ready for the cake to go in. The exception here, of course, is if you are going to chill something – perhaps a pastry – before you bake it, in which case, leave this step until indicated in the recipe. Also prepare your tins now before you start.

Measuring and mixing The next step is to measure out your ingredients. If they are going to be mixed, they can go in the same bowl – most scales allow you to return the weight to zero before you add the next ingredient.

Once the ingredients are mixed, spoon your batter into your prepared tins and pop them in the oven. Set the timer for about 10 minutes before

the cake is due to be ready – or around 20 per cent of the cooking time – and wait! Don't be tempted to open the oven door until you think the cake is ready.
Finishing While the cake is cooking, wash up and tidy up. It's much better to do it now, while you can enjoy the smell of the cake in the oven.

When your cake is ready, turn it out to cool and admire your handiwork.

MAKING MISTAKES

Everyone has successes and less-than-successes, so don't worry if things go wrong from time to time. You can usually disguise the problem – take a look at the tips on page 22 – and, if not, the birds will enjoy the fruits of your labours!

SEPARATING EGGS

To separate the white from the yolk, have two bowls ready. Crack the egg, then tip the yolk into one half of the shell, allowing the white to drop into one of the bowls. Tip the yolk into the other half of the shell, and continue until the egg white has all dropped away. Then put the yolk in the other bowl.

WHISKING

The idea of whisking is to introduce as much air as possible into the mixture, so use a wide bowl and a hand or electric whisk. With a hand whisk, use a wide circular motion, lifting your whisk out of the mixture as you work.
Whisking egg whites Always use a clean, grease-free whisk and bowl or the whites won't fluff up. They should go frothy and increase in volume until they form soft peaks when you lift out the whisk. Once that happens, stop whisking and go on to the next stage.

If you are adding sugar, do so gradually, whisking all the time until the mixture is glossy. If you pour sugar in one go onto whisked egg whites, you'll flatten them.

Whipping cream Use the same technique to whip double or whipping cream until it is thick and stands in peaks when you lift out the whisk. Don't overbeat or it will start to separate.

BEATING

This is just vigorous mixing of ingredients, with a hand whisk or wooden spoon. Take note of whether it is important not to work the mixture too hard.

Beating eggs and sugar You often beat eggs and sugar together at the beginning of a cake-making process. Use an electric mixer, if you have one, and beat until the mixture goes pale and light, and trails off the whisk in ribbons when you lift it out of the bowl.

FOLDING

When adding light ingredients, such as egg whites, to a mixture, first add a small quantity of the egg white to make the mixture lighter and looser. Then cut through the middle of the mixture with a metal spoon and fold the spoon round the edge so the ingredients are mixed together gently.

RUBBING IN

This is the technique of mixing butter into flour. Lift small amounts of the mixture and rub it through your fingertips until the mixture resembles coarse breadcrumbs. You can also use a pastry blender or pulse the mixture in a food processor.

MELTING CHOCOLATE

Always melt chocolate very gently or it will go grainy and spoil; there's not much you can do to rectify that. Place a heatproof bowl over a pan of gently simmering water, making sure the water is not touching the bowl. Break the chocolate into the bowl and stir occasionally until it is almost melted. Remove the bowl from the pan and continue to stir until it is all melted.

LINING CAKE TINS

If you don't use ready-made tin liners, here's
how to line a tin.

1. Cut a strip of baking paper about
6cm/2½in taller than the tin and long
enough to go all the way round. Cut a
circular piece to fit the base.

2. Fold the strip up 3cm/1¼in along the long edge (like the hem on a dress)
then snip at 2.5cm/1in intervals from the edge towards the fold.

3. Grease the cake tin.

4. Press the strip around the edge of the tin so that the cut strip is on the base.
Place the circle over the base of the tin.

BAKING BLIND

If the pastry case for a tart is going to need longer cooking than the filling, it must
be baked before the filling is added. Cover the uncooked pastry lining the baking
tin with a sheet of baking paper or greaseproof paper and fill with baking beans
to stop the base rising. Bake for the length of time given in the method, then
remove the paper and beans and either continue to bake the empty case or fill
and bake straight away.

WHEN IS A CAKE COOKED?

This is something you will learn with experience. Keep an eye on the cake while
it is cooking, but don't keep opening the oven door; most ovens now have a
glass window. When you think the cake is ready, take a look. The cake will be
well risen and will look golden and firm on top. If you press the centre lightly
with your finger, it should spring back. The edges of the cake will also start to
shrink away from the sides of the tin. You can test a cake by inserting a skewer
or sharp knife in the centre – it should come out clean.

Notes on the Recipes

✳ ✳ ✳ ✳ ✳ ✳ ✳ ✳

Take a look at these notes before you start baking any of the recipes so that you are familiar with the style and presentation of the book.

✳ The recipes generally make 4 servings, but the size of cake is indicated at the beginning of the recipe.

✳ Eggs, fruit and vegetables are medium unless otherwise stated.

✳ The recipes give metric and imperial measurements. It is advisable to follow only one set of measures.

✳ The ingredients are listed in the order in which they are used.

✳ All spoon measurements are level: 1 tsp = 5ml; 1 tbsp = 15ml.

✳ Wash fresh foods before use.

✳ Can and packet sizes are approximate and will depend on the particular brand.

✳ Taste the food as you cook and adjust the flavours to suit your own taste. Use your discretion in substituting ingredients and personalizing the recipes.

✳ Use whichever kitchen gadgets you like to speed up preparation and cooking times. An electric hand mixer will be the most useful item for both beating and whisking, or you can use a food processor, which is also perfect for grating, slicing, mixing or kneading.

✳ All ovens vary, so cooking times have to be approximate. Keep an eye on the oven while you are baking and adjust cooking times and temperatures to suit your appliance.

STORAGE & FREEZING

❉ Once cakes are completely cold, store them in an airtight container, or in the fridge if they contain fresh cream or other fresh ingredients.

❉ Most of the recipes are suitable for freezing. Cool completely, then wrap in clingfilm and seal in a freezer box or bag. Label with the name of the item and the date. Storage times are about 4 months.

❉ Leave to defrost naturally in the bag; this will take a couple of hours for cakes, or an hour or so for individual cakes.

❉ Do not freeze assembled cakes containing fruit layers, such as Black Forest Gâteau; cakes containing almond paste; no-bake melted bars; royal icing; and flapjacks. These are marked with a ❄ next to the recipe.

CONVERSIONS

If you need to convert your own recipe measurements, you might find these conversions useful. Note that cup measures are based on volume rather than weight, so one cup of any food may not weigh the same as another food. For example, a cup of flour weighs 100g/4oz, while a cup of butter weighs 225g/8oz.

WEIGHT

Metric	Imperial	Cups
25–30g	1oz	
50g	2oz	
75g	3oz	
100g	4oz	1 cup dried ingredients such as flour
150g	5oz	
175g	6oz	1 cup dried fruit or pulses
200g	7oz	
225g	8oz	1 cup fat or sugar
250g	9oz	
350g	12oz	
450g	1lb	

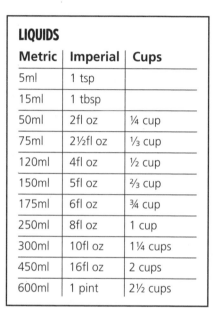

LIQUIDS

Metric	Imperial	Cups
5ml	1 tsp	
15ml	1 tbsp	
50ml	2fl oz	¼ cup
75ml	2½fl oz	⅓ cup
120ml	4fl oz	½ cup
150ml	5fl oz	⅔ cup
175ml	6fl oz	¾ cup
250ml	8fl oz	1 cup
300ml	10fl oz	1¼ cups
450ml	16fl oz	2 cups
600ml	1 pint	2½ cups

LENGTH

Metric	Imperial
2.5cm	1in
5cm	2in
10cm	4in
13cm	5in
15cm	6in
20cm	8in
25cm	10in
30cm	12in
35cm	14in
40cm	16in
45cm	18in

OVEN TEMPERATURES

Metric	Imperial	Gas mark	Metric	Imperial	Gas mark
110°C	225°F	gas ¼	190°C	375°F	gas 5
120°C	250°F	gas ½	200°C	400°F	gas 6
140°C	275°F	gas 1	220°C	425°F	gas 7
150°C	300°F	gas 2	230°C	450°F	gas 8
160°C	325°F	gas 3	240°C	475°F	gas 9
180°C	350°F	gas 4			

Troubleshooting

✳ ✳ ✳ ✳ ✳ ✳ ✳ ✳

Even experienced cooks have problems from time to time, so don't despair. Here are some imaginative solutions to common problems you may encounter with your baking.

The cake didn't rise You may not have included enough baking powder or egg, or the oven may have been too cool. Use it in a trifle.

The cake sank in the middle You could have used too much baking powder, making the cake rise too quickly and then sink. You may have taken it out of the oven before it was ready, or left the mixture standing before it went into the oven. If the cake tastes good, cut it before you serve and sprinkle with icing sugar to disguise the shape, or fill it with fruit or whipped cream before serving.

The base is burnt The oven was too hot or your baking tin too thin. Slice off the burnt portion, cut the cake in half horizontally and sandwich the two pieces together with some cream or buttercream.

The top is burnt If the top goes brown before the cake is cooked in the middle, the oven is too hot. Turn it down slightly, cover the top of the cake with a double piece of baking paper and return it to the oven to finish cooking.

The fruit sank Next time, toss the fruit in flour before stirring it in.

The cake tastes dry You may have overcooked the cake or not added quite enough liquid. If you have stored it, make sure your tins are airtight. Serve it warm with custard, or slice through horizontally and sandwich with buttercream.

The top is cracked The oven temperature is too high, or the oven shelf is too high.

The sponge is heavy This is usually the result of over-beating the mixture.

The cake is very crumbly This is usually caused by too much fat or not enough egg. Serve it with custard and a spoon.

The cake has risen unevenly You may not have mixed the batter properly, your tin may be uneven or your oven temperature is not constant throughout the oven. If it is the latter, you'll need to turn your cake tins as they bake.

CHAPTER 2

****

CUPCAKES, MUFFINS & other neat treats

Many of us make these cakes when we are children, and they always retain a special place in our repertoire; they're often the ones we go back to again and again. Easy to freeze and quick to defrost, they can be taken out of the freezer in ones or twos as you need them. Here are some traditional favourites and interesting newcomers for you to enjoy.

Your first cakes

✳ ✳ ✳ ✳ ✳ ✳ ✳ ✳

Many people have memories of making cakes when they were very young and it was just another game – one with something good to eat at the end. Those cakes were almost certainly a basic all-in-one.

The best place to start is usually at the beginning, so if you're taking up baking, or you want to teach your children how to make cakes – or even if you just need to keep them amused for an afternoon – this is the place to be. These little cakes are made with the simplest methods, kids love having their very own individual cakes, and if you are decorating them, each one can be a unique work of art!

You may want to run through the instructions for beginners on page 15 before you start, just to refresh your memory. It's always best to do something simple and to do it really well, so try to choose a recipe that you know is at the right level. None of the cakes in this section is complicated, so you have plenty of scope.

When it comes to doing the decorating, be adventurous. Choose a buttercream icing for simplicity, and collect as many fun things as you can to sprinkle or arrange on top: silver dragees, sugar strands, chocolate or jelly sweets, grated chocolate. Really go to town and make some splendid and unique cakes.

Fairy-wing Cakes

❋ ❋ ❋ ❋ ❋ ❋ ❋ ❋

This is perhaps the simplest recipe of all – but you can't beat it!
These little cakes look so pretty with their fairy wings on the top,
and they never go out of fashion.

INGREDIENTS *Makes 12 cupcakes*
150g/5oz plain flour
150g/5oz butter, softened
150g/5oz caster sugar
1 tsp baking powder
2 eggs, lightly beaten
FOR THE ICING
1 quantity Vanilla Buttercream
   (page 152)
2 tbsp sugar strands (optional)

METHOD
1. Preheat the oven to 180°C/350°F/
gas 4 and line a 12-hole cupcake tin
with paper cases.
2. Put all the cake ingredients into
a bowl and beat until well blended.
Spoon into the paper cases.
3. Bake in the oven for 10–15
minutes until risen and golden on
top. Transfer to a wire rack to cool
while you make the icing.
4. When the cupcakes are cold, slice
off the tops horizontally, then cut the
tops in half so you have 2 semi-circles.
Spread the icing over the top of the
cakes, then gently press the wings
into the icing at a 45-degree angle.
Sprinkle with sugar strands, if
you like.

BAKE WITH THE KIDS
These are great cakes to bake
with the kids. There's very little
that can go wrong, so they are
sure not to be disappointed
with the results.

Coffee Cupcakes

✽ ✽ ✽ ✽ ✽ ✽ ✽ ✽

With a subtle hint of coffee flavour, these are great for a mid-morning or afternoon snack and are also ideal for a child's lunch box treat – or an adult's, come to that.

INGREDIENTS *Makes 12 cupcakes*

150g/5oz plain flour
2 tbsp instant coffee granules
150g/5oz butter, softened
150g/5oz caster sugar
1 tsp baking powder
2 eggs, lightly beaten
2 tbsp milk (optional)

METHOD

1. Preheat the oven to 180°C/350°F/ gas 4 and line a 12-hole cupcake tin with paper cases.

2. Put the flour into a mixing bowl then rub the coffee granules through a sieve into the bowl.

3. Add all the remaining ingredients except the milk and beat until well blended. The mixture should be soft enough to drop off the spoon in lumps – if it feels a bit stiff, beat in the milk. Spoon the mixture into the paper cases.

4. Bake in the oven for 10–15 minutes until risen and golden on top. Transfer to a wire rack to cool.

Triple Chocolate Cupcakes

✳ ✳ ✳ ✳ ✳ ✳ ✳ ✳

There are not many people who don't enjoy a chocolate cake, so here are some with three chocolate choices! Use plain, milk and white chocolate chips, or chop up a bar of chocolate.

INGREDIENTS *Makes 12 cupcakes*

100g/4oz plain flour
50g/2oz cocoa powder
150g/5oz butter, softened
150g/5oz caster sugar
1 tsp baking powder
2 eggs, lightly beaten
100g/4oz chocolate chips
1 quantity Chocolate Buttercream
  (page 152)

METHOD

1. Preheat the oven to 180°C/350°F/ gas 4 and line a 12-hole cupcake tin with paper cases.
2. Put all the cake ingredients except the chocolate chips into a bowl and beat until well blended. Stir in the chocolate chips, then spoon into the paper cases.
3. Bake in the oven for 10–15 minutes until risen and golden on top. Transfer to a wire rack to cool while you make the icing.
4. You can simply swirl a generous spoonful of icing on top of the cakes. Alternatively, slice the top off each cake, spread with icing, then pop the top back on at a jaunty angle.

Creamy Iced Cupcakes

✳ ✳ ✳ ✳ ✳ ✳ ✳ ✳

Introducing a little whipped cream as well as the icing gives these cakes an extra touch of luxury, but you can easily leave out one or other, if you prefer.

INGREDIENTS *Makes 12 cupcakes*

150g/5oz plain flour
150g/5oz butter, softened
150g/5oz caster sugar
1 tsp baking powder
2 eggs, lightly beaten
1 tsp vanilla extract

FOR THE FILLING

4 tbsp strawberry jam
150ml/5fl oz double or whipping
  cream
½ quantity Vanilla Glacé Icing
  (page 151)

3. Bake in the oven for 10–15 minutes until risen and golden on top. Transfer to a wire rack to cool.
4. Whip the cream until stiff and make the icing.
5. When the cakes are cold, slice off the tops horizontally. Place 1 tsp of jam on top of each cake and spoon the cream on top. Replace the lids, then drizzle the icing over the top of the cakes.

METHOD

1. Preheat the oven to 180°C/350°F/ gas 4 and line a 12-hole cupcake tin with paper cases.
2. Put all the cake ingredients into a bowl and beat until well blended. Spoon into the paper cases.

Blueberry Muffins

Blueberry muffins are in the top ten favourite flavours. The added plus is that blueberries are a superfood, full of nutrients, so these aren't quite as self-indulgent as other muffins!

INGREDIENTS *Makes 12 muffins*

100g/4oz blueberries
225g/8oz plain flour
100g/4oz caster sugar
2 tsp baking powder
a pinch of salt
250ml/8fl oz milk
120ml/4fl oz sunflower oil
1 egg

METHOD

1. Preheat the oven to 200°C/400°F/gas 6 and line a 12-hole muffin tin with paper cases.

2. Sprinkle the blueberries with a little of the flour and toss together to coat lightly.

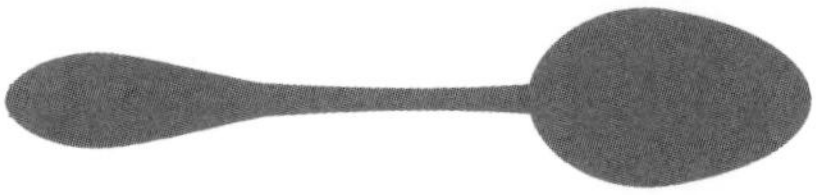

TAKE IT EASY

Do not overmix muffins or they will be tough and chewy.

3. Place the remaining flour in a bowl with the sugar, baking powder and salt. Make a well in the centre.

4. Pour the milk and oil into a jug. Break in the egg and gently mix them together.

5. Pour the liquid ingredients into the flour and stir together quickly, using a large spoon, until you cannot see any dry patches of flour but the batter is still lumpy. Gently fold in the blueberries. Spoon into the paper cases.

6. Bake in the oven for 20 minutes until well risen and golden on top. Transfer to a wire rack to cool.

Chocolate Chip Muffins

Use whichever type of chocolate chip you like – they will all work well. Chocolate chunks are good, too, or if you have a bar of chocolate, simply chop it into pieces.

INGREDIENTS *Makes 12 muffins*

225g/8oz plain flour
100g/4oz soft brown sugar
2 tsp baking powder
250ml/8fl oz milk
120ml/4fl oz sunflower oil
1 egg
150g/5oz chocolate chips or chunks

METHOD

1. Preheat the oven to 200°C/400°F/gas 6 and line a 12-hole muffin tin with paper cases.

2. Place the flour, sugar and baking powder in a bowl and make a well in the centre.

3. Pour the milk and oil into a jug. Break in the egg and gently mix them together.

4. Pour the liquid ingredients into the flour and stir together quickly, using a large spoon, until you cannot see any dry patches of flour but the batter is still lumpy. Gently fold in the chocolate chips. Spoon into the paper cases.

5. Bake in the oven for 20 minutes until well risen and firm on top. Transfer to a wire rack to cool.

COOK'S TIP

Most recipes make enough mixture to fill a 12-hole muffin tin. However, if you would like really large muffins, simply make 10 instead of 12.

Oat & Honey Muffins

These muffins have a lovely chewy texture with the distinctive sweetness of the honey. If you use a flower honey, it will have a particularly strong flavour. Search out local honey to combat hay fever.

INGREDIENTS *Makes 12 muffins*

100g/4oz plain flour
100g/4oz oatmeal
2 tsp baking powder
100g/4oz clear honey
250ml/8fl oz milk
100ml/3½fl oz sunflower oil
1 egg
2 tbsp rolled oats

METHOD

1. Preheat the oven to 200°C/400°F/gas 6 and line a 12-hole muffin tin with paper cases.
2. Place the flour, oatmeal and baking powder in a bowl and make a well in the centre.
3. Pour the honey, milk and oil into a jug. Break in the egg and gently mix them together.
4. Pour the liquid ingredients into the flour and stir together quickly, using a large spoon, until you cannot see any dry patches of flour but the batter is still lumpy. Spoon into the paper cases and sprinkle with the rolled oats.
5. Bake in the oven for 20 minutes until well risen and golden brown on top. Transfer to a wire rack to cool.

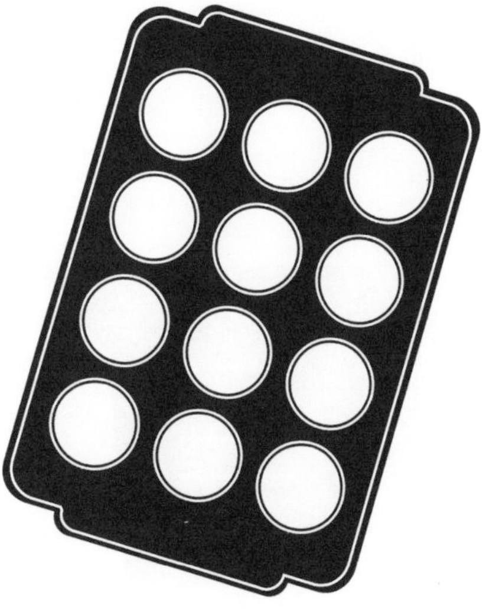

Toffee & Date Muffins

✤ ✤ ✤ ✤ ✤ ✤ ✤ ✤

I love toffee and caramel flavours, along with succulent fruits!
So here is a muffin recipe that is among my favourites – I hope you
like it as much as I do.

INGREDIENTS *Makes 12 muffins*

225g/8oz plain flour
100g/4oz soft dark brown sugar
2 tsp baking powder
a pinch of salt
150ml/5fl oz milk
100ml/3½fl oz canned caramel
120ml/4fl oz sunflower oil
1 egg
50g/2oz stoned dates, chopped
2 tbsp demerara sugar

METHOD

1. Preheat the oven to 200°C/400°F/
gas 6 and line a 12-hole muffin tin
with paper cases.
2. Place the flour, sugar, baking
powder and salt in a bowl and make
a well in the centre.
3. Pour the milk, caramel and oil into
a jug. Break in the egg and gently
mix them together.
4. Pour the liquid ingredients into
the flour and stir together quickly,
using a large spoon, until you cannot
see any dry patches of flour but the
batter is still lumpy. Gently fold in the
dates. Spoon into the paper cases and
sprinkle the tops with demerara sugar.
5. Bake in the oven for 20 minutes
until well risen and golden on top.
Transfer to a wire rack to cool.

Rock Cakes

✳ ✳ ✳ ✳ ✳ ✳ ✳

This is such a simple recipe and there's very little that can go wrong, so it's a great one for beginners or when you are short of time and just need something foolproof.

INGREDIENTS *Makes 12 cakes*
225g/8oz plain flour
3 tsp baking powder
100g/4oz butter
50g/2oz caster sugar
100g/4oz sultanas
50g/2oz raisins
1 egg, lightly beaten
1 tbsp milk
3 tbsp demerara sugar

METHOD
1. Preheat the oven to 200°C/400°F/ gas 6 and grease a baking sheet.
2. Place the flour and baking powder in a bowl. Rub in the butter until the mixture resembles coarse breadcrumbs. Stir in the sugar, sultanas and raisins.
3. Add the egg and mix together to a firm but not too stiff dough, adding some or all of the milk if necessary.

Drop spoonfuls of the mixture on to the prepared baking sheet and sprinkle with demerara sugar.
4. Bake in the oven for 15 minutes until well risen and golden on top. Transfer to a wire rack to cool.

Doughnuts

✳ ✳ ✳ ✳ ✳ ✳ ✳ ✳

Ring doughnuts are endlessly popular with everyone, and children especially love them. They take a little while to make but are well worth the effort.

INGREDIENTS *Makes 16 doughnuts*

300ml/10 fl oz warm milk
25g/1oz fresh yeast
50g/2oz caster sugar
450g/1lb strong plain flour,
  plus extra for dusting
a pinch of salt
50g/2oz butter
1 egg, lightly beaten
oil for deep-frying

FOR THE COATING

100g/4oz caster sugar
1 tsp ground cinnamon

METHOD

1. Pour the milk into a bowl and add the yeast and 1 tsp of the sugar. Whisk in 100g/4oz of the flour, then leave in a warm place until the mixture begins to bubble.

2. Mix the remaining flour and sugar with the salt, then rub in the butter until the mixture resembles breadcrumbs.

3. Whisk in the egg and the yeast mixture and mix to a soft dough.

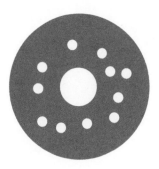

FAST-ACTION DRIED YEAST

If you use fast-action dried yeast, rub the butter into the flour and salt. Stir in the sugar and 1 sachet of yeast, then mix to a dough with the egg and warm milk.

Knead until smooth and no longer sticky. Cover with oiled clingfilm and leave in a warm place for 1 hour to rise.

4. Knead the dough again until smooth, then roll out to a thickness of 2cm/¾ in. Use a 7.5cm/3in cutter to cut into rings, then a 4cm/1½in cutter to cut out the centres. Arrange on a greased tray, cover and leave in a warm place for 20 minutes to rise.

5. Heat oil for deep-frying to 190°C/ 375°F. If you don't have a thermometer, have a few cubes of day-old bread handy. When you think the oil is hot enough, drop in a cube. It should brown in about 25 seconds. Carefully lower 3 doughnuts into the oil and fry for about 5 minutes until golden. Lift out on to kitchen paper to drain.

6. Bring the oil back to the correct temperature, then cook the remaining doughnuts a few at a time.

7. Mix the sugar and cinnamon in a bag, drop in 1 or 2 doughnuts at a time and shake to coat in the sugar.

Rich Egg Scones

❄ ❄ ❄ ❄ ❄ ❄ ❄ ❄

These are lovely scones that are ideal for a traditional Cornish cream tea. A pot of unsalted butter, some fresh clotted cream and a pot of jam make it complete. The scones are best served the day they are made.

INGREDIENTS *Makes 12 scones*

225g/8oz plain flour, plus extra
    for dusting
2 tsp baking powder
50g/2oz butter
25g/1oz caster sugar
1 egg, lightly beaten
120ml/4fl oz milk

METHOD

1. Preheat the oven to 220°C/425°F/ gas 7 and grease a baking sheet.
2. Put the flour, baking powder and butter in a bowl and rub in the butter until the mixture resembles coarse breadcrumbs.
3. Stir in the sugar, then mix in the egg and gradually add about 100ml/3½fl oz of the milk until you have a soft dough. Knead lightly until no longer cracked – do not overwork it.

4. Roll the dough out on a lightly floured surface to about 1.5cm/½in thick and cut into rounds with a 7.5cm/3in cookie cutter. Arrange on the prepared baking sheet and brush with the remaining milk.
5. Bake in the oven for 10 minutes until well risen and golden. Transfer to a wire rack to cool.

CHAPTER 3

✳✳✳✳✳✳✳✳

TRAYBAKES

This section is dedicated to cakes that are suited to a square or rectangular format. Many of them will work well in round cake tins, too, if you prefer – although strangely enough we do get used to particular cakes being one shape or another!

Bring on the family

✳ ✳ ✳ ✳ ✳ ✳ ✳ ✳

These cakes seem particularly suited to family cooks: you can cut them into different sizes for different appetites, they fit cake boxes and lunch boxes, they don't waste freezer space, and they're great for cake sales.

If you have a family, you'll be trying to cater for different tastes and appetites, and traybakes can really help here. For a start, they make it much easier to tailor your slice sizes to the members of the family, such as big chunks for teenage boys and smaller ones for the younger kids. Of course, they are also the right shape for plastic boxes for storage – if they last that long – and lunch boxes are generally square, too, so a slice can find its way into the lunch box as a treat.

If you like to keep a few things in the freezer for when you just don't have the time to cook, here's another plus: no wasted space like there often is around circular cakes.

Finally, once your children start school, it won't be long before you are sending in cakes to the cake sale or the school fête and many of these traybakes have been tried and tested in that context over the years.

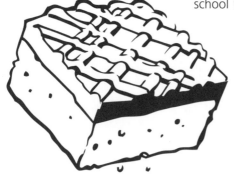

In fact, it's quite surprising that we choose to make round cakes at all!

Treacle & Cranberry Flapjacks

If you like treacle, you'll love the intense flavour of these crumbly flapjacks. Dried cranberries make a useful addition to the storecupboard and are a nice change from raisins.

INGREDIENTS *Makes 8 bars*
200g/7oz butter
75g/3oz soft dark brown sugar
50g/2oz black treacle
250g/9oz rolled oats
75g/3oz dried cranberries

METHOD
1. Preheat the oven to 180°C/350°F/ gas 4 and grease and line a 20cm/8in square cake tin.

2. Melt the butter, sugar and treacle in a pan over a low heat until soft, then stir in the oats and cranberries. Spoon into the prepared tin and press down gently.

3. Bake in the oven for about 20 minutes until shiny and going slightly brown.

4. Leave to cool in the tin for 5 minutes, then cut into squares while still warm. Cool for another 5 minutes in the tin, then transfer to a wire rack while they are just slightly warm but beginning to firm up.

PIZZA WHEEL
It is much easier to use a pizza wheel to cut flapjacks, although you may need a knife to get to the edges.

Millionaire's Shortbread

❊ ❊ ❊ ❊ ❊ ❊ ❊ ❊

There are three mouth-watering layers in this delicious traybake:
shortbread, caramel and chocolate. Some people call it
'rich man's shortbread'.

INGREDIENTS *Makes 12 squares*

FOR THE BASE
300g/11oz plain flour
100g/4oz caster sugar
225g/8oz butter

FOR THE FILLING
225g/8oz butter
225g/8oz soft light brown sugar
4 tbsp golden syrup
400g/14oz can condensed milk
a few drops of vanilla extract

FOR THE TOPPING
350g/12oz dark chocolate

METHOD

1. Preheat the oven to 200°C/400°F/
gas 6 and grease and line a
20cm/8in square cake tin.
2. Put the flour in a bowl with the
sugar and rub in the butter until the
mixture resembles breadcrumbs.
Keep kneading until the mixture
forms a soft dough. Press into the
base of the prepared tin and prick
with a fork.

3. Bake in the oven for 25 minutes, then leave the shortbread base to cool in the tin.

4. To make the filling, put all the filling ingredients except the vanilla into a pan and stir over a low heat until the sugar has melted. Bring to the boil, then simmer for 7 minutes, stirring continuously.

5. Remove from the heat, add the vanilla and beat the mixture thoroughly until smooth and thick. Pour over the base and leave to set.

6. Melt the chocolate in a heatproof bowl over a pan of gently simmering water. Pour over the caramel filling and leave to cool and set before cutting into squares.

Nut & Apricot Traybake

✤ ✤ ✤ ✤ ✤ ✤ ✤ ✤

This is an upside-down cake, baked with the topping on the base so that you turn it out to reveal a shiny, fruity layer. Make sure you turn it out while it is warm as it is much less likely to stick.

INGREDIENTS *Makes 12 bars*
FOR THE TOPPING
100g/4oz almonds
100g/4oz ready-to-eat dried apricots
50g/2oz butter
50g/2oz soft light brown sugar
FOR THE CAKE
100g/4oz plain flour
50g/2oz ground almonds
175g/6oz butter
175g/6oz soft light brown sugar
2 tsp baking powder
3 eggs, lightly beaten
1 tsp almond extract

METHOD
1. Preheat the oven to 160°C/325°F/gas 3 and grease and line a 20×25cm/8×10in cake tin.
2. To make the topping, sprinkle the almonds and apricots over the base of the tin. Melt the butter and sugar for the topping in a small pan, then pour the mixture over the fruit and nuts.
3. In a bowl, mix together all the cake ingredients until smooth, then spoon them over the topping.
4. Place in the oven and bake for 1 hour until springy to the touch. Leave to cool in the tin for just a few minutes, then carefully invert the tin onto a board. Lift off the tin and carefully remove the lining paper, using a palette knife to press back any of the topping that lifts off as you do so. Leave to cool completely, then cut into bars.

Coffee Gingerbread

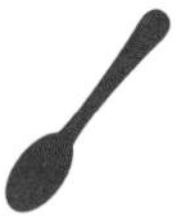

This is a lovely, light cake, a golden russet colour with the delicious aroma and flavour of coffee. Make sure you dissolve the coffee completely so the flavour permeates the cake.

INGREDIENTS *Makes 12 bars*

2 tsp instant coffee granules
100ml/3½fl oz hot water
100g/4oz butter
50g/2oz soft light brown sugar
75g/3oz golden syrup
175g/6oz plain flour
2 tsp baking powder
2 tsp ground ginger
2 eggs, lightly beaten

METHOD

1. Preheat the oven to 180°C/350°F/gas 4 and grease and line a 20×30cm/8×10in cake tin.

2. Dissolve the coffee in the hot water.

3. Melt the butter, sugar and syrup in a pan over a low heat, stirring occasionally. Remove from the heat as soon as they are blended.

4. Put the flour, baking powder and ginger in a bowl, then stir in the melted mixture, followed by the coffee and eggs. Spoon into the prepared tin.

5. Bake in the oven for 40 minutes until well risen and slightly springy to the touch.

6. Leave to cool in the tin for 5 minutes, then turn out to finish cooling on to a wire rack.

Sticky Gingerbread

This recipe is a very old friend – I can't imagine how many I have made. It comes in many different variations but the traditional one is probably the one I like best, very moist and gooey.

INGREDIENTS *Makes 12 bars*

150g/5oz black treacle
150g/5oz golden syrup
100g/4oz butter
100g/4oz soft dark brown sugar
275g/10oz plain flour
2 tsp baking powder
1 tsp ground cinnamon
1 tsp ground ginger
2 eggs, lightly beaten
1 tsp bicarbonate of soda
150ml/5fl oz hot water

METHOD

1. Preheat the oven to 180°C/350°F/gas 4 and grease and line a 20×30cm/8×10in baking tin.
2. Melt the treacle, syrup, butter and sugar in a pan over a low heat, stirring occasionally. Remove from the heat as soon as they are blended.
3. Put the flour, baking powder, cinnamon and ginger in a bowl, then stir in the melted mixture, followed by the eggs, bicarbonate of soda and hot water. Spoon into the prepared tin.
4. Bake in the oven for 45 minutes until well risen and firm to the touch.
5. Leave to cool in the tin for 5 minutes, then turn out to finish cooling on to a wire rack.

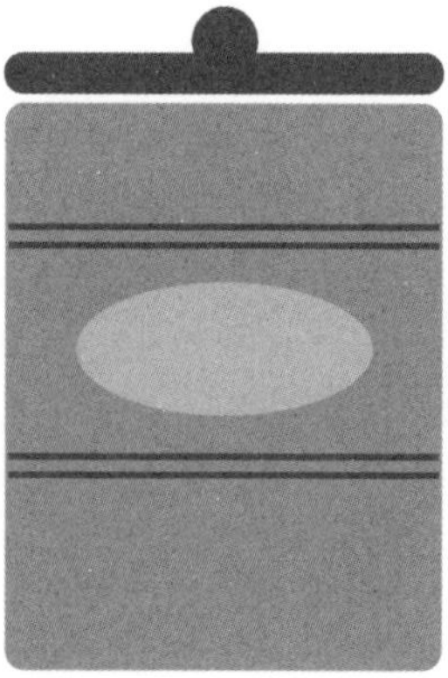

Parkin

❊ ❊ ❊ ❊ ❊ ❊ ❊ ❊

An old Yorkshire recipe, parkin improves if you keep it well wrapped in an airtight tin for a few days before you eat it. It seems to improve the flavour and texture.

INGREDIENTS *Makes 8 bars*

225g/8oz butter
200g/7oz golden syrup
100g/4oz soft dark brown sugar
50g/2oz black treacle
200g/7oz plain flour
150g/5oz oatmeal
2 tsp baking powder
4 tsp ground ginger
2 tsp freshly grated nutmeg
1 tsp mixed spice
2 eggs, lightly beaten
3 tbsp milk

METHOD

1. Preheat the oven to 140°C/275°F/ gas 1 and grease and line a 20cm/8in square cake tin.
2. Melt the butter, syrup, sugar and treacle in a pan over a low heat, stirring occasionally. Remove from the heat as soon as they are blended.

3. Put the flour, oatmeal, baking powder and spices in a bowl, then stir in the melted mixture, followed by the eggs and milk. Spoon into the prepared tin.
4. Bake in the oven for 1½ hours until firm and a rich brown. Leave to cool in the tin.

Hello Dolly Traybake

This is a version of an American recipe given to me by a friend who was living near Boston. It's very different in style from traditional English recipes.

INGREDIENTS *Makes 8 bars*

100g/4oz butter
100g/4oz digestive biscuit crumbs
100g/4oz chocolate chips
50g/2oz coconut flakes or desiccated coconut
100g/4oz chopped walnuts
400g/14oz can of condensed milk

METHOD

1. Preheat the oven to 180°C/350°F/gas 4 and grease and line a 20×30cm/8×12in cake tin.

2. Melt the butter in a pan and stir in the biscuit crumbs. Spoon into the prepared tin and press into the base.

3. Sprinkle with the chocolate chips, then the coconut and walnuts. Pour the condensed milk over.

4. Bake in the oven for 25 minutes until golden on top.

5. Leave to cool in the tin for 5 minutes, then cut into squares while still warm and loosen around the edges. Leave for another 5 minutes, then transfer to a wire rack while still slightly warm.

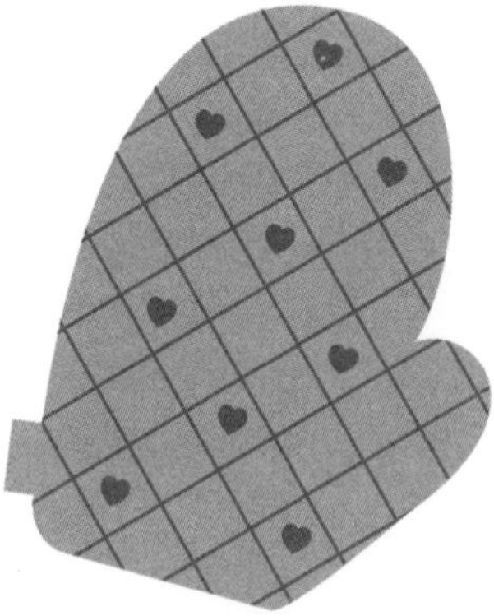

Chocolate & Orange Marble Bars

✳ ✳ ✳ ✳ ✳ ✳ ✳ ✳

Marble cakes look very special when you cut through the cake, although they are simplicity itself to make. You simply colour and flavour two halves of the mixture and swirl them together in the tin.

INGREDIENTS *Makes 8 bars*

225g/8oz butter
225/8oz caster sugar
3 eggs, lightly beaten
225g/8oz plain flour
2 tsp baking powder
1 tsp vanilla extract
grated zest and juice of 1 orange
3 tbsp cocoa powder
2 tbsp milk (optional)

METHOD

1. Preheat the oven to 180°C/350°F/ gas 4 and grease and line a 20×30cm/8×12in cake tin.

2. In a bowl, beat together the butter and sugar until pale and creamy. Gradually beat in the eggs, flour, baking powder, vanilla and orange zest and juice so you have a soft, creamy mixture.

3. Divide the mixture in half. Mix the cocoa powder into one half, adding a little of the milk if the mixture appears too thick. Place large spoonfuls of the mixtures alternately into the prepared tin, then swirl lightly with a fork to make a marble pattern.

4. Bake in the oven for 35 minutes until risen and springy to the touch.

5. Leave to cool in the tin for 5 minutes, then turn out to finish cooling on a wire rack.

Ginger & Sultana Traybake

This is a lovely spicy traybake made with plenty of ginger, which I think is a particularly warming spice. Don't waste the syrup from the jar of stem ginger, even when you've finished the ginger – just use it in your baking.

INGREDIENTS *Makes 12 bars*

100g/4oz butter
100g/4oz soft light brown sugar
2 eggs
100g/4oz plain flour
1½ tsp baking powder
50g/2oz sultanas
50g/2oz chopped mixed nuts
2 balls stem ginger, chopped
1 tbsp ginger syrup from the jar
2 tbsp demerara sugar

METHOD

1. Preheat the oven to 180°C/350°F/gas 4 and grease and line a 20×25cm/8×10in cake tin.

2. In a bowl, beat together the butter and sugar until pale and creamy.

3. Gradually beat in the eggs, then mix in all the remaining ingredients except the demerara sugar. Spoon the mixture into the prepared tin and sprinkle with the demerara.

4. Bake in the oven for 30 minutes until well risen and springy to the touch.

5. Leave to cool in the tin for 5 minutes, then turn out to finish cooling on a wire rack.

Chocolate Banana Squares

❊ ❊ ❊ ❊ ❊ ❊ ❊ ❊

Banana cakes have a familiar dense texture. This one adds chocolate, making it a little different. If you have a food processor, this is an ideal recipe for putting everything in the bowl and pressing the button.

INGREDIENTS *Makes 8 bars*

150g/5oz caster sugar
100g/4oz butter
2 small, ripe bananas, mashed
2 eggs
225g/8oz plain flour
2 tsp baking powder
50g/2oz drinking chocolate powder
4 tbsp milk

BANANA CAKES

Cakes made with banana tend to have a moist and quite dense texture. They are very tasty, last well, and are a great way to use up any leftover ripe bananas.

METHOD

1. Preheat the oven to 180°C/350°F/ gas 4 and grease and line a 20cm/8in square cake tin.
2. Beat together the sugar and butter until smooth and creamy. Beat in the bananas until well mixed.
3. Add the eggs and mix in well; this mixture will look curdled. Then add the dry ingredients and the milk and mix until blended. Spoon into the prepared tin.

4. Bake in the oven for 1 hour until firm. Check by inserting a skewer in the centre – it should come out clean.
5. Leave to cool in the tin for 5 minutes, then turn out to finish cooling on a wire rack.

Honey-frosted Pineapple Pulp Cake

This is for those who have juicers and don't like to waste the pulp, although do make sure you have peeled your pineapple before you juice it. If you don't have juicer pulp, blend some fresh or canned pineapple.

INGREDIENTS

Makes a 20cm/8in cake

150g/5oz pineapple pulp
150g/5oz plain flour
2 tsp baking powder
100g/4oz caster sugar
150ml/5fl oz sunflower oil
2 eggs

FOR THE FROSTING

100g/4oz cream cheese
4 tbsp honey
a pinch of freshly grated nutmeg

METHOD

1. Preheat the oven to 160°C/325°F/gas 3 and grease and line a 20cm/8in cake tin.

2. Mix all the cake ingredients in a bowl and beat until well blended. Turn into the prepared tin.

3. Bake in the oven for 30 minutes until golden and firm to the touch.

4. Leave to cool in the tin for 5 minutes, then turn out to finish cooling on a wire rack.

5. To make the frosting, simply beat together the cream cheese, honey and nutmeg until you have a smooth icing and spread it over the top and sides of the cake.

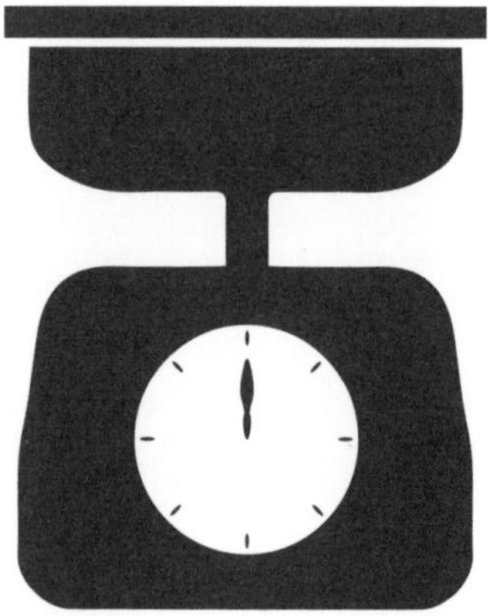

Strawberry & Coconut Traybake

✳ ✳ ✳ ✳ ✳ ✳ ✳ ✳

This makes a layered cake with a soft inside, so is best eaten quickly otherwise it can go soggy. You could also serve it with cream as a dessert.

INGREDIENTS

Makes a 20cm/8in cake ❄
100g/4oz butter
50g/2oz caster sugar
2 eggs, lightly beaten
100g/4oz plain flour
1 tbsp baking powder
120ml/4fl oz milk
100g/4oz desiccated coconut
150g/5oz strawberries, halved
   if large
1 tbsp demerara sugar

METHOD

1. Preheat the oven to 180°C/350°F/ gas 4 and grease and line a 20cm/8in cake tin.

2. In a bowl, beat together the butter and sugar until pale and creamy.

3. Add the eggs, flour, baking powder, milk and half the coconut and mix until smooth.

4. Spoon half the mixture into the prepared tin, sprinkle with the strawberries and top with the remaining mixture. Sprinkle with the remaining coconut and the demerara sugar.

5. Bake in the oven for 30 minutes until golden brown and springy to the touch.

6. Leave to cool in the tin for 5 minutes, then turn out to finish cooling on a wire rack.

Sugared Date Traybake

✳ ✳ ✳ ✳ ✳ ✳ ✳ ✳

Lovely and spicy with a sugared top and a cake dotted with dates, this makes a delicious treat at any time of day. The cinnamon and nutmeg give it a warming lift.

INGREDIENTS *Makes 12 bars*

100g/4oz butter
225g/8oz soft light brown sugar
2 eggs
175g/6oz plain flour
½ tsp bicarbonate of soda
½ tsp ground cinnamon
½ tsp freshly grated nutmeg
¼ tsp ground cloves
a pinch of salt
175g/6oz dates, stoned and chopped
2 tbsp demerara sugar

METHOD

1. Preheat the oven to 180°C/350°F/ gas 4 and grease and line a 20×25cm/8×10in cake tin.

2. In a bowl, beat together the butter and sugar until pale and creamy.

3. Beat in the eggs one at a time. Mix in all the remaining ingredients except the demerara sugar and beat until well blended. Spoon into the prepared tin and sprinkle with the demerara sugar.

4. Bake in the oven for 25 minutes until a skewer inserted in the centre comes out clean. Leave to cool in the tin.

CHAPTER 4

✳✳✳✳✳✳✳✳

SPONGES & PLAIN CAKES

From the classic sponge cake to a feather-light angel cake,
you can dress these cakes up – adding cream or buttercream
fillings and frostings – or keep them simple and stylish.

Keep it simple

❊ ❊ ❊ ❊ ❊ ❊ ❊

There's no need to overcomplicate cakes. For a really special occasion you may want to pull out all the stops, but letting good-quality ingredients speak for themselves is often the best way to enjoy them.

Round, square, rectangular or baked in a loaf tin, these are cakes that are classics, each one focusing on a particular flavour and showing it off at its best. Take the Crystal-top Lemon Drizzle Cake (page 59), for example. When you taste the sharp tang of the fresh lemon juice, you'll be in no doubt as to what is being showcased on that particular plate.

Some of these are traditionally English cakes – and you can't get much more English than a Classic Victoria Sponge (page 56). Others offer more unusual options, such as the Hungarian Rice Cake (page 65) – and there is also the quintessentially American Angel Cake (page 60), made with just egg whites so it is both as light and as white as a feather.

Serve these delicate cakes on their own; they look great on the best china plates! They also lend themselves well to being served with some delicate fruits, such as soft strawberries with the Angel Cake and slices of orange with the Tunisian Orange Cake (page 58).

Some of the cakes can be frosted, if you like, but they are usually left plain, perhaps dusted with a little icing sugar, shaken over the top through a fine sieve.

DOILY PATTERNS

To make a pattern in icing sugar on a cake, put a doily on the top, shake the icing sugar over, then carefully remove the doily. It works best if the pattern is quite simple, so why not try making your own stencil?

All-in-one Sandwich Cake

✳ ✳ ✳ ✳ ✳ ✳ ✳ ✳

An all-in-one cake takes only minutes to make, especially in a food processor. Purists say that this method does not produce such a light result as a creamed cake, but it works well for me!

INGREDIENTS

Makes a 20cm/8in cake

175g/6oz plain flour
2 tsp baking powder
175g/6oz butter, softened
175g/6oz caster sugar
3 eggs, lightly beaten
½ tsp vanilla extract
a little icing sugar, sifted

FOR THE FILLING

75g/3oz raspberry jam
250ml/8fl oz double or
    whipping cream

METHOD

1. Heat the oven to 160°C/325°F/ gas 3 and grease and line two 20cm/8in cake tins.
2. Beat all the ingredients except the icing sugar together in a large bowl until you have a smooth mixture. Spoon into the prepared tins.

3. Bake in the oven for about 30 minutes until golden and springy to the touch.
4. Leave to cool in the tin for 5 minutes, then turn out to finish cooling on a wire rack.
5. Spread one cake with the jam. Whip the cream until stiff, then spread over the jam and top with the remaining cake. Serve sprinkled with icing sugar.

Classic Victoria Sponge

❊ ❊ ❊ ❊ ❊ ❊ ❊ ❊

*Dusted with icing sugar and sandwiched with whipped cream
and strawberry jam, a Victoria sponge cannot be beaten for
understated elegance.*

INGREDIENTS

Makes a 20cm/8in cake
175g/6oz butter
175g/6oz caster sugar
3 eggs, lightly beaten
175g/6oz plain flour
1 tsp baking powder
75g/3oz strawberry jam
250ml/8fl oz double or
    whipping cream
a little icing sugar, sifted

METHOD

1. Heat the oven to 190°C/375°F/
gas 5 and grease and line two
20cm/8in sandwich tins.

2. In a bowl, beat together the
butter and sugar until pale and
creamy. The mixture should trail off
the whisk in ribbons.

3. Gradually add the eggs, a little
at a time, adding a spoonful of the
flour between each addition. Then
whisk in the remaining flour and
baking powder, keeping the mixture
as light as possible. Spoon into the
prepared tins.

4. Bake in the oven for about
20 minutes until golden and springy
to the touch.

5. Leave to cool in the tin for a few
minutes, then turn out to finish
cooling on a wire rack.

6. Spread the jam over the top of
one of the cakes. Whip the cream
until stiff, then spread it over the
jam. Put the second cake on top and
sprinkle with icing sugar.

Madeira Cake

✳ ✳ ✳ ✳ ✳ ✳ ✳ ✳

This is another popular classic, which is lovely with a glass of Madeira, the sweet Spanish wine – or indeed with a cup of tea – when you can take the time to sit down and make the most of it.

INGREDIENTS

Makes a 900g/2lb cake
175g/6oz butter
175g/6oz caster sugar
3 eggs, lightly beaten
150g/5oz self-raising flour
100g/4oz plain flour
a pinch of salt
grated zest and juice ½ lemon

MADEIRA

Madeira cake is named after the sweet, fortified wine with which it was often served in Britain during the 18th and 19th centuries.

METHOD

1. Heat the oven to 160°C/325°F/ gas 3 and grease and line a 900g/2lb loaf tin.
2. In a large bowl, beat together the butter and sugar until pale and creamy.

3. Gradually add the eggs, a little at a time, adding a spoonful of the flour between each addition. Then whisk in the remaining flour, the salt, and the lemon zest and juice. Spoon into the prepared tin.
4. Bake in the oven for 1 hour until golden and springy to the touch.
5. Leave to cool in the tin for 10 minutes, then turn out to finish cooling on a wire rack.

Tunisian Orange Cake

❊ ❊ ❊ ❊ ❊ ❊ ❊ ❊

Luscious and rich with the flavours of North Africa, this is a flourless cake made with ground almonds and breadcrumbs, soaked in a citrus syrup.

INGREDIENTS

Makes a 23cm/9in cake
6 eggs, lightly beaten
250ml/8fl oz sunflower oil
200g/7oz caster sugar
100g/4oz ground almonds
50g/2oz breadcrumbs
2 tsp baking powder
grated zest and juice of 1 orange

FOR THE SYRUP

100g/4oz caster sugar
juice of 1 lemon
juice of 1 orange

METHOD

1. Heat the oven to 180°C/350°F/ gas 4 and grease and line a 23cm/9in cake tin.
2. In a large bowl, lightly beat the eggs with the oil. Add the remaining cake ingredients and mix well. Spoon into the prepared tin.

3. Bake in the oven for 40 minutes until golden and springy to the touch.
4. Meanwhile, put the syrup ingredients in a pan and heat gently until the sugar has melted. Boil rapidly for 4 minutes until you have a thick syrup.
5. Leave the cake in the tin and pierce the top in several places. Spoon the syrup over and leave to cool.

Crystal-top Lemon Drizzle Cake

The mixture of demerara sugar and lemon syrup that you pour on the top makes a lovely crunchy crust and adds to the sharp lemon tang in the sponge.

INGREDIENTS

Makes a 900g/2lb loaf cake

100g/4oz butter

175g/6oz caster sugar

2 eggs, lightly beaten

175g/6oz plain flour

2 tsp baking powder

4 tbsp milk

grated zest of 1 lemon

2 tbsp demerara sugar

FOR THE SYRUP

45g/1½oz icing sugar, sifted

4 tbsp lemon juice

METHOD

1. Heat the oven to 180°C/350°F/ gas 4 and grease and line a 900g/2lb loaf tin.

2. In a large bowl, beat together the butter and sugar until pale and creamy.

3. Gradually add the eggs alternately with the flour and baking powder, then beat in the milk and lemon zest to create a soft mixture that easily drops off the end of the spoon. Spoon into the prepared tin and sprinkle with the demerara.

4. Bake in the oven for 40 minutes until golden brown and springy to the touch.

5. Mix together the icing sugar and lemon juice to create a syrup. As soon as you take the cake out of the oven, pierce the top several times with a skewer, then spoon the syrup over the top so that it soaks into the cake. Leave to cool in the tin.

Angel Cake

As light as a feather and beautifully white, angel cake is made with egg whites so it is almost fat-free and extremely light, which makes it quite a rarity among cakes.

INGREDIENTS

Makes a 23cm/9in cake
8 egg whites, at room temperature
150g/5oz caster sugar
a pinch of salt
1 tsp cream of tartar
1 tsp vanilla extract
100g/4oz plain flour
75g/3oz icing sugar, sifted
225g/8oz strawberries, blackcurrants
   and blackberries

METHOD

1. Heat the oven to 180°C/350°F/ gas 4 and grease a 23cm/9in ring pan or cake tin.

2. Put the egg whites in a large, clean bowl and whisk with an electric whisk until frothy.

3. Add the caster sugar, salt, cream of tartar and vanilla extract and continue whisking until the mixture forms stiff peaks when you lift out the whisk.

4. Gently fold in the flour and icing sugar using a metal spoon. Spoon into the prepared tin and tap the tin gently to pop any air bubbles.

5. Bake in the oven for about 30 minutes until the cake springs back when you gently press it in the centre.

6. Turn the cake upside down on to a wire rack and leave to cool before you loosen the edges with a knife and remove it from the tin. Serve with the soft fruits.

Marmalade Cake

If you love the tangy flavour of marmalade – especially the chunky, beautifully bitter, home-made kind – you'll love this rugged cake with its slightly sharp flavour.

INGREDIENTS

Makes a 20cm/8in cake

175g/6oz butter
90ml/3fl oz golden syrup
2 eggs, lightly beaten
75g/3oz orange marmalade
350g/12oz plain flour
1 tbsp baking powder
1 tsp ground cinnamon
1 tsp freshly grated nutmeg
a pinch of ground cloves
150ml/5fl oz milk

FOR THE TOPPING

2 tbsp golden syrup
100g/4oz orange marmalade
50g/2oz rice flake cereal

METHOD

1. Heat the oven to 180°C/350°F/ gas 4 and grease and line a 20cm/8in square cake tin.

2. Beat the butter and syrup until soft and creamy. Beat in the eggs and marmalade.

3. Add the flour, baking powder and spices and continue to beat, gradually adding enough milk until everything is well mixed and you have a fairly stiff cake mixture. Spoon into the prepared tin.

4. Mix together the topping ingredients and spoon over the cake.

5. Bake in the oven for about 1 hour until the top is crispy and a knife inserted into the centre comes out clean. Transfer to a wire rack to cool.

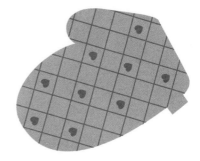

Meringue-topped Milk Cake

✳ ✳ ✳ ✳ ✳ ✳ ✳ ✳

This unusual cake has a thin layer of meringue on the top, covering a layer of jam and a light sponge cake. Slivered almonds on top give it crunch.

INGREDIENTS

Makes a 20cm/8in cake ❄

100g/4oz butter

100g/4oz caster sugar

2 eggs, separated

100g/4oz plain flour

2 tsp baking powder

1 tsp vanilla extract

3 tbsp condensed milk or milk

FOR THE TOPPING

2 egg whites

25g/1oz caster sugar

4 tbsp jam

2 tbsp flaked almonds

METHOD

1. Heat the oven to 180°C/350°F/ gas 4 and grease and line a 20cm/8in cake tin.

2. In a large bowl, beat together the butter and sugar until pale and creamy.

SEPARATING EGGS

To separate an egg, hold the egg over a bowl and crack the shell. Lift off one half, keeping the egg yolk in the other half. Tip the yolk from one half shell to the other, allowing the white to fall into the bowl. Tip the yolk into a separate bowl.

3. Blend in the egg yolks, flour, baking powder, vanilla extract and condensed milk.

4. Whisk the egg whites until stiff. Using a metal spoon, fold a spoonful into the cake mixture to make it lighter, then fold in the remaining egg whites. Spoon into the prepared tin.

5. Bake in the oven for 30 minutes until well risen and golden, and a skewer inserted in the centre comes out clean.

6. Remove the cake from the oven and leave to cool in the tin for a few minutes while you prepare the topping. Reduce the oven temperature to 160°C/325°F/gas 3.

7. Whisk the egg whites until stiff. Gradually fold in the sugar, using a metal spoon, and continue whisking until stiff and shiny.

8. Spread the cake with the jam, keeping it about 1cm/¾in from the edge, then spoon the meringue roughly over the cake and sprinkle with the flaked almonds. Return the cake to the oven for a further 20 minutes.

Caramel Cake

✳ ✳ ✳ ✳ ✳ ✳ ✳ ✳

I usually make this in a square tin as it is easier to divide into pieces for the lunch box. Some cakes only seem to look right when they are round, but this one works both ways.

INGREDIENTS

Makes a 20cm/8in cake
150g/5oz caster sugar
100g/4oz butter
2 eggs, lightly beaten
150g/5oz plain flour
1 tsp baking powder
100g/4oz canned caramel

FOR THE CARAMEL BUTTERCREAM

50g/2oz canned caramel
50g/2oz unsalted butter
100g/4oz icing sugar, sifted

METHOD

1. Heat the oven to 160°C/325°F/ gas 3 and grease and line a 20cm/8in square or round cake tin.
2. In a large bowl, beat the sugar and butter until pale and creamy.
3. Gradually beat in the eggs alternately with the flour and baking powder, then beat in the caramel until you have a smooth mixture. Spoon it into the prepared tin.
4. Bake in the oven for 30 minutes until well risen and springy to the touch. Leave to cool in the tin for a few minutes, then turn out to finish cooling on a wire rack.
5. To make the buttercream, beat all the ingredients together until pale and creamy. Spread roughly over the top of the cake.

Hungarian Rice Cake

❋ ❋ ❋ ❋ ❋ ❋ ❋ ❋

This light cake is sometimes baked with added raisins. It is gluten-free, so it is suitable for those who cannot eat wheat and other gluten-containing cereals.

INGREDIENTS

Makes a 23cm/9in cake
250g/9oz short-grain rice
1.2 litres/2 pints milk
30g/1oz butter
5 eggs, separated
75g/3oz caster sugar
grated zest of 1 lemon
15g/½oz icing sugar, sifted

METHOD

1. Put the rice and milk in a heavy-based pan, bring to a simmer, then simmer gently for 35 minutes until soft and creamy. Stir in the butter and leave to cool to room temperature.
2. Heat the oven to 180°C/350°F/ gas 4 and grease and line a 23cm/9in springform cake tin.
3. Lightly beat the egg yolks, sugar and lemon zest until pale, then stir into the rice.

4. Whisk the egg whites until stiff. Using a metal spoon, stir a few spoonfuls of the egg white into the rice mixture to loosen it, then lightly fold in the remainder. Spoon into the prepared pan.
5. Bake in the oven for 45 minutes until a skewer inserted in the centre comes out clean.
6. Leave to cool in the tin for 5 minutes, then turn out to finish cooling on a wire rack. Serve sprinkled with icing sugar.

Caraway Seed Cake

✢ ✢ ✢ ✢ ✢ ✢ ✢ ✢

*This is a traditional cake to make around harvest time in the autumn.
Caraway seeds have quite an intense flavour, so don't add too many.
The whisked egg whites make the cake very light.*

INGREDIENTS

Makes a 900g/2lb loaf cake
175g/6oz butter
175g/6oz caster sugar
1 tbsp caraway seeds
3 eggs, separated
250g/9oz plain flour
25g/1oz ground almonds
1½ tsp baking powder
2 tbsp milk (optional)
1 quantity Lemon Glacé Icing
   (page 151) (optional)

METHOD

1. Heat the oven to 180°C/350°F/
gas 4 and grease and line a 900g/2lb
loaf tin.
2. In a large bowl, beat together
the butter and sugar until pale and
creamy. Stir in the caraway seeds.
3. Whisk the egg whites until just
stiff. Lightly beat the egg yolks.

4. Fold the yolks into the butter
and sugar mixture, then fold in the
flour, almonds and baking powder.
Finally, lightly fold in the egg whites,
using a metal spoon, until everything
is blended. Add a little milk if the
mixture is too dry. Spoon into the
prepared tin.
5. Bake in the oven for about 1 hour
until firm to the touch. Leave to cool
in the tin for 5 minutes, then turn
out to finish cooling on a wire rack.
6. Cover with lemon icing to finish,
if liked.

Swiss Roll

A light and airy jam-filled roll, this will taste so much better than the one from the corner shop! The cake will break a little when you roll it, but that's part of its charm.

INGREDIENTS

Makes a 20cm/8in roll
75g/3oz self-raising flour
a pinch of salt
3 eggs
75g/3oz caster sugar
1 tbsp hot water

FOR ROLLING AND FILLING
3 tbsp caster sugar
100g/4oz strawberry jam
1 tbsp icing sugar, sifted

METHOD

1. Heat the oven to 220°C/425°F/ gas 7 and grease and line a 20×30cm/8×12in Swiss roll tin.
2. Sift the flour and salt into a bowl.
3. Whisk the eggs and sugar in a heatproof bowl set over a pan of simmering water until pale. Remove from the heat.
4. Gradually fold in the flour and hot water. Spoon into the prepared tin.
5. Bake in the oven for 10 minutes until golden and springy to the touch.
6. Sprinkle a sheet of baking paper with the sugar.
7. Turn the cake upside-down on to the paper, trim the edges and remove the lining. Spread with jam, roll up and leave to cool.

CREAM FILLING

If you want to fill the roll with buttercream or jam and cream, do not remove the lining paper. Roll the cake up around the paper and leave to cool. When cold, unroll, spread carefully with jam and cream, then roll up again.

Scandinavian Cake

✳ ✳ ✳ ✳ ✳ ✳ ✳ ✳

Serve this plain but tasty cake with some fresh berries and a scoop of ice cream. Choose your fruits according to the season; strawberries, raspberries or blackberries will all go well.

INGREDIENTS

Makes a 23cm/9in cake
100g/4oz butter
175g/6oz plain flour
5 eggs
300g/11oz caster sugar
1½ tsp baking powder
a pinch of salt
1 tsp almond extract

METHOD

1. Heat the oven to 160°C/325°F/ gas 3 and grease and line a 23cm/9in cake tin.

2. Beat the butter and flour with an electric mixer for 4–5 minutes.

3. Add the eggs one at a time, beating well and making sure all the mixture is blended. Add the remaining ingredients and beat thoroughly until well blended. Spoon into the prepared cake tin.

4. Bake in the oven for 1 hour until well risen and springy to the touch.

5. Leave to cool in the tin for 5 minutes, then turn out to finish cooling on a wire rack.

CHAPTER 5

* * * * * * * *

CHOCOLATE CAKES

Nearly everyone loves a chocolate cake, so here's a wide selection.
Among other delights, you'll find chocolate teamed with fudge,
brandy and even a pinch of chilli for a South American touch.

Chocoholic heaven

✳ ✳ ✳ ✳ ✳ ✳ ✳ ✳

The arguments rage about whether chocolate is good for us or not, whether it releases the feel-good endorphins or just makes us put on weight! Let common sense rule, I say – just don't eat too much.

If you love chocolate, there's nothing like it for making you feel better, crowning a special occasion or rounding off a lovely meal. You don't need the science to know it tastes wonderful, enhances your spirits when you are happy and gives you a boost when you are down.

You also know you have to be a little cautious about how much you allow yourself to eat before that healthy balanced diet and five-a-day of all the right things goes right out of the window! But that's true of all sweet things – they are meant to be a treat, not something we eat at every meal, so enjoy chocolate in moderation.

That makes it even more important to choose the best chocolate, and you will find that chocolate with more than 70 per cent cocoa solids will make a real difference to the flavour of your chocolate cakes. It will make them rich and intense – just much more chocolatey! The ingredients may cost a little more but it will be well worth it.

When you are melting chocolate, take note of the tips on page 17. It is vital to melt it very gently so as not to overheat it, and you must take care that water doesn't get into it. In either case, the chocolate will go grainy and will be spoiled.

 Easy All-in-one Chocolate Cake

✳ ✳ ✳ ✳ ✳ ✳ ✳

I have made versions of this cake more times than I can remember and it has never let me down – the name tells you everything you need to know.

INGREDIENTS

Makes a 20cm/8in cake

200g/7oz plain flour

20g/¾oz cocoa powder

1 tsp bicarbonate of soda

1 tsp baking powder

150g/5oz caster or soft light
   brown sugar

2 tbsp golden syrup

2 eggs, lightly beaten

150ml/5fl oz milk

150ml/5fl oz sunflower oil

VARIATIONS

You can also bake the cake in two 18cm/7in tins, then sandwich them together with whipped cream or buttercream (page 152), either plain or chocolate. Top with buttercream or Rich Chocolate Icing (page 154), or simply dust with a little icing sugar.

METHOD

1. Heat the oven to 160°C/325°F/ gas 3 and grease and line a 20cm/8in cake tin. (Do not use a loose-based cake tin as this makes quite a liquid batter.)

2. Stir all the dry ingredients together in a large bowl and make a well in the centre.

3. Add the syrup, eggs, milk and oil and beat together until you have a shiny, quite thin cake mix. Spoon into the prepared tin.

4. Bake in the oven for 35 minutes until well risen and springy to the touch.

5. Leave to cool in the tin for a few minutes, then turn out to finish cooling on a wire rack.

Chocolate Roulade

❄ ❄ ❄ ❄ ❄ ❄ ❄ ❄

This is the perfect recipe for making your Christmas yule log.
Light and delicious, it can be rolled round buttercream or whipped
cream. You could even try chocolate spread and cream.

INGREDIENTS

Makes a 20cm/8in roll
50g/2oz self-raising flour
25g/1oz cocoa powder
a pinch of salt
3 eggs
75g/3oz caster sugar
1 tbsp hot water

FOR ROLLING AND FILLING

3 tbsp caster sugar
1 quantity Chocolate Buttercream
  (page 152)
1 tbsp icing sugar, sifted

METHOD

1. Heat the oven to 220°C/425°F/
gas 7 and grease and line a
20x30cm/8x12in Swiss roll tin.
2. Sift the flour, cocoa and salt into
a bowl.
3. Put the eggs and sugar in a
heatproof bowl set over a pan of
simmering water and whisk until
the mixture is pale and trails off the
whisk in ribbons. Remove from the
heat. Gradually fold in the flour a
little at a time, with the hot water.
Spoon into the prepared tin, tilting
the tin so it spreads evenly.
4. Bake in the oven for 10 minutes
until springy to the touch.
5. While it is baking, spread a sheet
of baking paper on the worktop and
sprinkle with the sugar.
6. Turn the cake upside-down
straight out on to the paper, peel off
the lining paper and trim off the crisp
edges of the cake. Roll up from the
short edge, using the paper to help,
then place on a wire rack, cover with
a clean tea towel and leave to cool.
7. Once cool, gently unroll, spread
with buttercream, then roll up again.
Dust with icing sugar before serving.

Mud Pie

Rich, sticky and so chocolatey, this is a dieter's nightmare, so keep the slices thin. The texture is half way to a dense chocolate cheesecake, so it's best served with a spoon and fork.

INGREDIENTS

Makes a 20cm/8in cake
225g/8oz butter
225g/8oz dark chocolate
225g/8oz caster sugar
4 eggs, lightly beaten
1 tbsp cornflour

METHOD

1. Heat the oven to 180°C/350°F/ gas 4 and grease and line a 20cm/8in cake tin. Alternatively, simply grease a pie dish (such as a Pyrex dish) and serve the cake straight from the dish, which is easier than trying to turn out the sticky cake.

2. Melt the butter and chocolate gently over a low heat, then stir in the sugar. Remove from the heat and gradually mix in the eggs and fold in the cornflour. Spoon into the prepared dish.

3. Stand the dish in a large roasting tin and fill with boiling water to come halfway up the sides of the dish.

4. Bake in the oven for 1 hour. Leave to cool in the tin, then refrigerate until ready to serve.

BREAKING UP CHOCOLATE

If you need to break up a bar of chocolate, it is much easier to do it before you open the wrapper.

Chilli Chocolate Layer Cake

✸ ✸ ✸ ✸ ✸ ✸ ✸ ✸

The touch of chilli really brings this cake alive. It's an unusual flavour combination in Europe but comes from South America, where it has been used since Pre-Colombian times.

INGREDIENTS

Makes a deep 20cm/8in cake
450g/1lb caster sugar
200g/7oz plain flour
75g/3oz cocoa powder
1 tsp mild chilli powder
2 tsp bicarbonate of soda
1 tsp baking powder
a pinch of salt
250ml/8fl oz buttermilk
120ml/4fl oz sunflower oil
3 eggs
1 tsp vanilla extract
250ml/8fl oz hot coffee

FOR FILLING AND TOPPING
300ml/10fl oz double cream
50g/2oz dark chocolate

METHOD

1. Heat the oven to 180°C/350°F/ gas 4 and grease and line three 20cm/8in cake tins.

2. In a large bowl, mix the sugar, flour, cocoa, chilli powder, bicarbonate of soda, baking powder and salt and make a well in the centre.

3. In another bowl, mix the buttermilk, oil, eggs, vanilla and coffee together, then beat them into the flour mixture to make a quite liquid mixture. Spoon into the prepared tins.

4. Bake in the oven for 35 minutes until well risen and springy to the touch.

5. Leave to cool in the tin for 5 minutes, then turn out to finish cooling on a wire rack.

6. Whip the cream until stiff, then sandwich the cakes together with layers of cream.

7. Heat the chocolate in a heatproof bowl over a pan of simmering water until just melted, then swirl it over the cake.

Chocolate Rum Cakes

✳ ✳ ✳ ✳ ✳ ✳ ✳

*If you wish to you can replace the rum with your favourite tipple
in this grown-up cake that is childishly simple to make.
Use milk chocolate if you prefer.*

INGREDIENTS *Makes 12*

200g/7oz butter
200g/7oz dark chocolate
50g/2oz soft light brown sugar
250g/9oz sultana bran cereal
50g/2oz sultanas or raisins
50g/2oz hazelnuts, chopped
2 tbsp rum

METHOD

1. Line a 12-hole muffin tin with paper cases.
2. Melt the butter, chocolate and sugar in a pan over a very low heat.
3. Stir in the cereal, sultanas or raisins, hazelnuts and rum.
4. Spoon into the paper cases and chill until set.

A LARGER CAKE
You can make this in a 900g/1lb loaf tin and use a hot, serrated knife to cut it into chunks, but it does crumble at the edges so you have to cut big pieces.

Black Forest Gâteau

✢ ✢ ✢ ✢ ✢ ✢ ✢ ✢

The quintessential Eighties dessert, this extravagant chocolate and cherry creation is re-emerging in the 21st century as a popular cake once more.

INGREDIENTS

Makes a 20cm/8in cake

20g/¾oz cocoa powder
75ml/2½fl oz boiling water
250g/9oz butter
250g/9oz caster sugar
250g/9oz plain flour
2 tbsp baking powder

4 eggs, lightly beaten
400g/14oz can morello cherries
  in syrup
1 tsp cornflour
1 tbsp cold water
3 tbsp kirsch
450ml/15fl oz double cream
100g/4oz dark chocolate, grated

METHOD

1. Heat the oven to 180°C/350°F/ gas 4 and grease and line two 20cm/8in cake tins.

2. Dissolve the cocoa in the boiling water.

3. In a large bowl, beat together the butter, sugar, flour, baking powder and eggs until thoroughly blended. Beat in the cocoa. Spoon the mixture into the prepared tins.

4. Bake in the oven for 25 minutes until well risen and springy to the touch.

5. Leave to cool in the tin for 5 minutes, then turn out to finish cooling on a wire rack.

6. Drain the cherries and reserve 75ml/2½fl oz of the syrup. Reserve 12 cherries for decoration and halve the remainder.

7. Pour the syrup into a small pan and heat gently. Mix the cornflour and water to a paste, then whisk it into the syrup, bring to the boil, and boil for 2 minutes until thickened. Stir in 1 tbsp of the kirsch and leave to cool.

8. Slice the cakes in half horizontally and sprinkle them with the remaining kirsch.

9. Whip the cream until stiff, then spread one cake layer with about a quarter of the cream, sprinkle with a third of the cherries and drizzle with a spoonful of the syrup. Repeat with two more cake layers, then top with the final cake. Spread the remaining cream over the top and sides of the cake. Press the grated chocolate into the cream and decorate with the reserved cherries.

Iced Chocolate Sponge

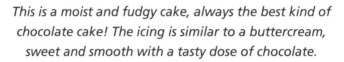

This is a moist and fudgy cake, always the best kind of chocolate cake! The icing is similar to a buttercream, sweet and smooth with a tasty dose of chocolate.

INGREDIENTS

Makes a 900g/2lb loaf cake

250ml/8fl oz water

120ml/4fl oz oil

100g/4oz butter

20g/¾oz cocoa powder

350g/12oz caster sugar

225g/8oz plain flour

2 tsp baking powder

2 eggs

½ tsp bicarbonate of soda

120ml/4fl oz milk

1 tsp vanilla extract

FOR THE ICING

20g/¾oz cocoa powder

100g/4oz butter

5 tbsp evaporated milk

450g/1lb icing sugar, sifted

1 tsp vanilla extract

METHOD

1. Heat the oven to 180°C/350°F/ gas 4 and grease and line a 900g/2lb loaf tin.

2. Put the water, oil, butter and cocoa in a saucepan and bring to the boil. Remove from the heat and stir in the sugar. Keep stirring until everything has dissolved. Stir in the flour and baking powder.

3. In a separate bowl, beat together the eggs, bicarbonate of soda, milk and vanilla, then stir into the butter mixture in the pan. Pour the mixture into the prepared tin.

4. Bake in the oven for about 1 hour until springy to the touch.

5. Leave to cool in the tin for 5 minutes, then turn out to finish cooling on a wire rack.

6. Beat the icing ingredients until smooth, then spread over the top.

Mocha Marble Cake

✤ ✤ ✤ ✤ ✤ ✤ ✤ ✤

Here chocolate and coffee flavours swirl together in one cake.
Although this is a very simple and easy-to-bake cake,
it is full of flavour and interest.

INGREDIENTS

Makes a 20×25cm/8×10in cake
200g/7oz butter
200g/7oz soft light brown sugar
4 eggs, lightly beaten
200g/7oz plain flour
1½ tsp baking powder
50g/2oz cocoa powder
100ml/3½fl oz milk
50g/2oz instant coffee granules,
   crushed

METHOD

1. Heat the oven to 180°C/350°F/
gas 4 and grease and line a
20×25cm/8×10in cake tin.
2. In a bowl, beat together the butter
and sugar until pale and creamy.
3. Beat in a little of the egg, then
a spoonful of flour, alternating
until the eggs, flour and baking
powder are incorporated.

4. Divide the mixture in half. Mix
the cocoa and half the milk into
one half, and the coffee and the
remaining milk into the other half.
5. Place large spoonfuls of each
mixture alternately into the prepared
tin, then pull a skewer through the
mixture to swirl them together.
6. Bake in the oven for 30 minutes until
well risen and springy to the touch.
7. Leave to cool in the tin for
5 minutes, then turn out to finish
cooling on a wire rack.

Devil's Food Cake

❄ ❄ ❄ ❄ ❄ ❄ ❄ ❄

If you don't go for the light and delicately white Angel Cake, perhaps this is more to your liking! It is a rich and dense chocolate cake with a delicious, sweet frosting.

INGREDIENTS

Makes a 23cm/9in cake
300ml/10fl oz milk
75g/3oz cocoa powder
300g/11oz granulated sugar
225g/8oz plain flour
1¼ tsp bicarbonate of soda
a pinch of salt
175g/6oz butter, diced
3 eggs, lightly beaten
1 tsp vanilla extract

FOR THE FROSTING
350g/12oz granulated sugar
75ml/2½fl oz milk
50g/2oz dark chocolate
1½ tbsp golden syrup
40g/1½oz butter, softened
a few drops of vanilla extract

METHOD

1. Heat the oven to 180°C/350°F/ gas 4 and grease and line two 23cm/9in sandwich tins.

2. In a small pan, bring the milk just to the boil, then whisk in the cocoa and 50g/2oz of the sugar until dissolved. Leave to cool.

3. In a large bowl, mix together the remaining sugar with the flour, bicarbonate of soda and salt. Add the butter and half the milk mixture and beat for about 3 minutes.

4. Add the eggs, vanilla and remaining milk and beat until well blended. Spoon the mixture into the prepared tins.

5. Bake in the oven for 30 minutes until well risen and springy to the touch.

6. Leave to cool in the tin for 5 minutes, then turn out to finish cooling on a wire rack.

7. To make the frosting, place the sugar, milk, chocolate and syrup in a pan over a medium heat and bring to the boil, stirring frequently. Reduce the heat and simmer until the syrup reaches 115°C/242°F or when a drop of the syrup turns to a soft ball when put into cold water. Do not stir.

8. Remove from the heat and beat in the butter and vanilla, then leave to cool for about 1 hour to room temperature.

9. Beat until the frosting becomes creamy, adding a few drops of hot water if it is too stiff.

10. Sandwich the cakes together with the frosting, or use two-thirds in between the cakes and one-third on top.

Gooey Chocolate & Cream Cake

*This is best served with a fork or a spoon as it is very moist and luscious and more than halfway to being a dessert –
it is self-indulgence at its finest!*

INGREDIENTS

Makes a 23cm/9in cake
100g/4oz dark chocolate
175g/6oz butter
200g/7oz caster sugar
5 eggs, lightly beaten
50g/2oz self-raising flour
200g/7oz chopped mixed nuts

TO SERVE

clotted cream, crème fraîche or
  vanilla ice-cream

METHOD

1. Heat the oven to 200°C/400°F/
gas 6 and grease and line a 23cm/9in
springform cake tin.
2. Melt the chocolate in a heatproof
bowl set over a pan of gently
simmering water.
3. In a bowl, beat the butter and
sugar until pale and creamy.
4. Beat the eggs into the butter and
sugar mixture one at a time. Beat in
the flour, then fold in the chocolate
and nuts. Spoon the mixture into the
prepared tin.
5. Bake in the oven for 35 minutes
until set but still very moist.
6. Leave to cool in the tin for
5 minutes, then turn out and serve
warm with clotted cream, crème
fraîche or ice-cream.

Chocolate Fudge Slice

✳ ✳ ✳ ✳ ✳ ✳ ✳ ✳

No book on cakes could be considered really complete without that modern-day favourite, the chocolate fudge cake. The ground almonds give a particularly moist touch.

INGREDIENTS

Makes a 20×25cm/8×10in cake
175g/6oz butter
125g/4½oz soft dark brown sugar
4 eggs, lightly beaten
150g/5oz plain flour
100g/4oz ground almonds
2 tsp baking powder
15g/½oz cocoa powder
2–3 tbsp milk (optional)
200g/7oz dark chocolate,
  finely chopped
150g/5oz fudge, cut into chunks

METHOD

1. Heat the oven to 160°C/325°F/ gas 3 and grease and line a 20×25cm/8×10in cake tin.
2. In a large bowl, beat the butter and sugar until light and creamy.
3. Gradually beat in the eggs alternately with the flour, ground almonds, baking powder and cocoa. Add some or all of the milk if the mixture feels too stiff. Fold in the chocolate, then the fudge. Spoon into the prepared tin.
4. Bake in the oven for 20 minutes until well risen and springy to the touch.
5. Leave to cool in the tin for a few minutes, then turn out to finish cooling on a wire rack. Serve warm or cold.

Chocolate Brownies

The chewy centre and crisp layer on the top are what makes brownies unique – and uniquely popular. They should never be dry, so make sure you don't overcook them.

INGREDIENTS *Makes 8*

200g/7oz demerara sugar
3 eggs
5 tbsp sunflower oil
1 tsp vanilla essence
100g/4oz plain flour
¼ tsp bicarbonate of soda
a pinch of salt
25g/1oz cocoa powder
25g/1oz drinking chocolate powder
100g/4oz pecan nuts, chopped

METHOD

1. Heat the oven to 180°C/350°F/ gas 4 and grease and line a 20cm/8in square cake tin.
2. In a bowl, beat together the sugar, eggs, oil and vanilla until well blended.
3. Beat in the remaining ingredients. Spoon the mixture into the prepared tin.

4. Bake in the oven for 30 minutes until just firm.
5. Leave to cool in the tin, then cut into bars or squares.

CHAPTER 6

* * * * * * * * *

FRUIT, VEGETABLE & NUT CAKES

As well as the ever-popular fruit cake, this section includes cakes made with carrots and courgettes, plus delicious nutty cakes, made with or without flour. This could alter your ideas on what a fruit and nut cake can be!

Nuts about fruit cake

✳ ✳ ✳ ✳ ✳ ✳ ✳

The variety of ingredients options available in this section is vast; from dried fruits to fresh, succulent vegetables, there is something for everyone.

Traditional fruit cakes have the great advantage that they keep really well, allowing you to have one in an airtight tin for any occasion that requires a slice of something rich and sweet.

But in this section, we look much further afield than just the sultana, raisin and currant variety of fruit cake. Home-grown fruits such as apples and damsons are featured, alongside fruits from hotter climes, such as pineapples, bananas and dates.

Vegetables were formerly used more often in cakes than they are now, but the famous Carrot Cake (page 103) had to be included in this chapter, along with the less frequently encountered Courgette Cake (page 104) and Pumpkin Cake (page 102).

And no cake book would be complete without including some nutty offerings, especially Hazelnut Cake (page 107), which could also feature in the gluten-free chapter as it contains no flour.

Christmas Mincemeat Cake

This simple cake is a great way to use up the half-full jar of mincemeat we all seem to be left with when we've had enough of mince pies over the season.

INGREDIENTS

Makes a 20cm/8in cake

150g/5oz butter
150g/5oz dark brown sugar
3 eggs, lightly beaten
200g/7oz plain flour
1 tsp baking powder
1 tsp mixed spice
1 tsp lemon juice
300g/11oz mincemeat

METHOD

1. Heat the oven to 180°C/350°F/gas 4 and grease and line a 20cm/8in cake tin.

2. Beat together the butter and sugar until pale and creamy.

3. Beat in a little of the egg, then a spoonful of flour, alternating until the eggs are incorporated. Mix in the remaining flour with the baking powder, spice and lemon juice. Stir in the mincemeat. Spoon into the prepared tin.

4. Bake in the oven for 30 minutes. Reduce the oven temperature to 160°C/325°F/gas 3 and bake for a further 20 minutes until well risen and firm to the touch. A skewer inserted in the centre should come out clean.

5. Leave to cool in the tin for 5 minutes, then turn out to finish cooling on a wire rack.

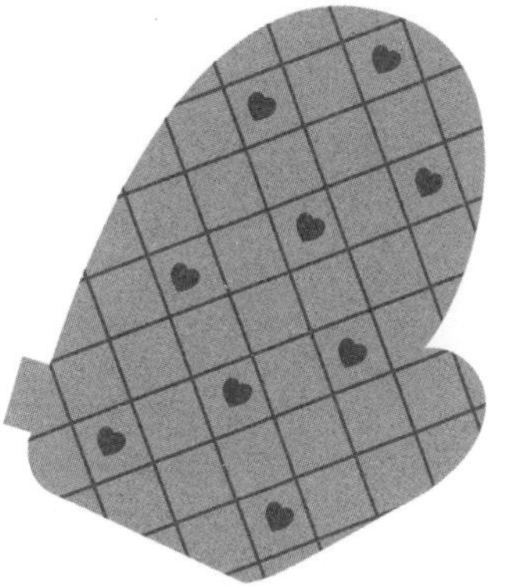

Christmas Cake

✳ ✳ ✳ ✳ ✳ ✳ ✳ ✳

This is a lovely, rich cake that is best made at least a couple of months in advance so that the flavours are fully developed by the time Christmas Day arrives.

INGREDIENTS

Makes a 25cm/10in cake
400g/14oz dried mixed fruit
400g/14oz sultanas
400g/14oz raisins
200g/7oz glacé cherries,
  roughly chopped
100ml/3½fl oz brandy or whisky
grated zest and juice of 1 lemon
300g/11oz plain flour
100g/4oz ground almonds
50g/2oz flaked almonds
1½ tsp baking powder
1½ tsp mixed spice
1 tsp ground cinnamon
½ tsp freshly grated nutmeg
¼ tsp ground cloves
250g/9oz butter
250g/9oz soft dark brown sugar
6 eggs
about 150ml/5fl oz milk

METHOD

1. Heat the oven to 150°C/300°F/ gas 2 and grease and line a 25cm/10in cake tin.
2. Mix the fruit, brandy and lemon zest and juice in a bowl and stir well.
3. Mix the flour, ground and flaked almonds, baking powder and spices in another bowl.
4. Beat together the butter and sugar until smooth and creamy.

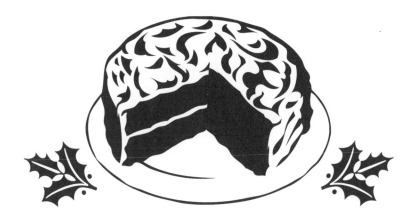

Gradually add the eggs, one at a time, beating continuously.

5. Stir the flour mixture into the butter mixture, then stir in the fruits, adding enough milk to give a soft, dropping consistency. Spoon into the prepared cake tin.

6. Bake in the oven for 1½ hours. Reduce the oven temperature to 120°C/250°F/gas ½ and cook for a further 2 hours until a skewer inserted in the centre comes out clean. Cover the top with foil if it appears to be browning too quickly.

7. Leave to cool in the tin for 15 minutes, then turn out to finish cooling on a wire rack.

8. Wrap the cake securely in foil, place it in a tin and leave to mature

YORKSHIRE STYLE

If you have never eaten a slice of Christmas cake with a wedge of creamy, crumbly Wensleydale cheese, then you are missing a treat. Do try this wonderful Yorkshire tradition.

in a cool, dark place. You can feed it periodically during maturation with a little more liquor. Open the cake tin and the top of the foil wrapping, pierce the top of the cake a few times with a skewer, then spoon in a little brandy or whisky and watch it soak into the cake. Seal it up again securely.

Simnel Cake

�֎ �֎ ✖ ✖ ✖ ✖ ✖ ✖

Traditionally made for Easter, simnel cake has a layer of almond paste through the centre and on the top, and is decorated with 11 almond paste balls to represent the 11 faithful disciples (without Judas Iscariot).

INGREDIENTS

Makes a 20cm/8in cake
225g/8oz butter
225g/8oz soft light brown sugar
grated zest of 2 lemons
4 eggs, separated
500g/1lb 2oz currants
175g/6oz sultanas
100g/4oz glacé cherries, chopped
75g/3oz chopped mixed peel
400g/14oz plain flour
1 tsp baking powder
1–2 tbsp milk
450g/1lb almond paste, bought or
    homemade (page 157)
a little icing sugar, for dusting
2 tbsp apricot jam
chocolate mini eggs or other
    Easter decorations

METHOD

1. Heat the oven to 180°C/350°F/ gas 4 and grease and line a 20cm/8in cake tin.

2. Beat together the butter, sugar and lemon zest until light and fluffy.

3. Gradually beat in the eggs, then mix in the fruit. Fold in the flour and baking powder, adding the milk if the mixture is too stiff.

4. Roll out one-third of the almond paste on a surface sprinkled with icing sugar and cut into a 20cm/8in round.

5. Spoon half the cake mixture into the prepared tin and level the surface. Top with the almond paste, then spoon in the remaining mixture.

6. Bake in the oven for 1 hour. Reduce the oven temperature to 200°C/150°F/gas 2 and bake for a further 3 hours until the cake is golden brown and a skewer inserted in the centre comes out clean. Leave to cool in the tin.

7. Roll out half the remaining almond paste and cut into a 20cm/8in round. Roll the remainder into 11 equal-sized balls.

8. Remove the cake from the tin and brush with a little of the apricot jam. Gently press the almond paste on top. Brush the top with jam and gently press the 11 balls equally around the edge, brushing them with jam. Flash under a hot grill for a few minutes until the tops of the balls are lightly browned.

9. Decorate with eggs or other Easter decorations to serve.

Stout Fruit Cake

❄ ❄ ❄ ❄ ❄ ❄ ❄ ❄

This is 'stout' as in rich, dark ale! If you can wrap the cake in foil and resist the temptation to eat it for a week or so, you will be rewarded with a more mature flavour.

INGREDIENTS

Makes an 18cm/7in cake
250g/9oz wholemeal flour
1 tsp baking powder
100g/4oz butter
100g/4oz soft light brown sugar
1 tsp mixed spice
grated zest of 1 lemon
150ml/5fl oz stout or dark ale
2 eggs, lightly beaten
100g/4oz raisins
100g/4oz prunes, stoned and
   chopped
100g/4oz currants

METHOD

1. Heat the oven to 180°C/350°F/ gas 4 and grease and line an 18cm/7in cake tin.
2. Put all the ingredients except the fruit in a bowl and beat until well blended. Stir in the fruit, then spoon the mixture into the prepared tin.
3. Bake in the oven for 1½ hours until well risen and firm to the touch.
4. Leave to cool in the tin for 5 minutes, then turn out to finish cooling on a wire rack.

Dundee Cake

A rich fruit cake, this has an almond topping and, not surprisingly because the clue is in the name, a dram of Scotch whisky to give it depth of flavour.

INGREDIENTS

Makes a 20cm/8in cake

250g/9oz butter
250g/9oz soft light brown sugar
4 eggs
375g/13oz plain flour
100g/4oz ground almonds
1 tsp baking powder
1 tsp mixed spice
grated zest and juice of 1 lemon
75ml/2½fl oz whisky
200g/7oz sultanas
200g/7oz raisins
100g/4oz glacé cherries, halved
150g/5oz almonds
1 tbsp honey, warmed

METHOD

1. Heat the oven to 160°C/325°F/gas 3 and grease and line a 20cm/8in cake tin.

2. Beat together the butter and sugar until pale and creamy.

3. Beat in a little of the egg, then a spoonful of flour, alternating until the eggs are incorporated. Mix in the remaining flour, together with the ground almonds, baking powder, mixed spice and lemon zest and juice. Stir in the whisky, sultanas, raisins and cherries.

4. Spoon into the prepared tin. Gently press the almonds in a concentric pattern on top of the cake.

5. Bake in the oven for 2½ hours, covering the top with baking paper or foil if it appears to be browning too quickly. The cake should be well risen and firm to the touch.

6. Leave to cool in the tin for 5 minutes, then turn out. Brush with the honey and leave to finish cooling on a wire rack.

Coconut, Pineapple & Carrot Cake

You might think this combination of ingredients could be overkill, but in fact it works well and creates a quite robust and certainly delicious cake with a lovely texture.

INGREDIENTS

Makes a 23cm/9in cake

350g/12oz caster sugar
300g/11oz butter
3 eggs
1 tsp vanilla extract
225g/8oz plain flour
1 tsp bicarbonate of soda
2 tsp ground cinnamon
225g/8oz carrots, grated
100g/4oz canned pineapple, drained and crushed
100g/4oz desiccated coconut
100g/4oz chopped mixed nuts
icing sugar, for sprinkling

METHOD

1. Heat the oven to 160°C/325°F/gas 3 and grease and line a 23cm/9in cake tin.

2. Beat together the sugar, butter, eggs and vanilla extract until smooth and creamy.

3. Gradually beat in the flour, bicarbonate of soda and cinnamon.

4. Fold in the carrots, pineapple, coconut and nuts. Spoon into the prepared tin.

5. Bake in the oven for 1¼ hours until the top is golden brown and a skewer inserted in the centre comes out clean.

6. Leave to cool in the tin for 5 minutes, then turn out to finish cooling on a wire rack.

Old-fashioned Pound Cake

✳ ✳ ✳ ✳ ✳ ✳ ✳ ✳

This cake was so named because all the main ingredients were originally in 1lb quantities. This is a scaled-down version on the same principle, making it quick to make and easy to remember.

INGREDIENTS

Makes a 20cm/8in cake

250g/9oz butter
250g/9oz caster sugar
4 eggs, lightly beaten
250g/9oz plain flour
250g/9oz raisins
250g/9oz sultanas
250g/9oz glacé cherries and
   mixed peel
1 tsp mixed spice
2 tbsp brandy

METHOD

1. Heat the oven to 150°C/300°F/
gas 2 and grease and line a
20cm/8in cake tin.
2. Beat together the butter and
sugar until pale and creamy.
3. Add the eggs one at a time,
beating well between each addition.
Fold in the flour, fruit, mixed spice
and brandy, then spoon into the
prepared tin.
4. Bake in the oven for 2½ hours
until the top is golden brown and a
skewer inserted in the centre comes
out clean. Cover with baking paper
or foil if it appears to be browning
too quickly.
5. Leave to cool in the tin for
20 minutes, then turn out to finish
cooling on to a wire rack.

Cherry & Coconut Cake

Coconut is a very popular flavour in cakes, and it helps to keep the mixture moist as well as sweet. You can chop the glacé cherries, if you prefer.

INGREDIENTS

Makes a 20cm/8in cake

175g/6oz butter

350g/12oz self-raising flour

225g/8oz glacé cherries, quartered

100g/4oz desiccated coconut

175g/6oz caster sugar

2 eggs, lightly beaten

200ml/7fl oz milk

METHOD

1. Heat the oven to 180°C/350°F/gas 4 and grease and line a 20cm/8in cake tin.

2. Rub the butter into the flour until the mixture resembles coarse breadcrumbs.

3. Toss the cherries in the coconut, then fold them into the mixture with the coconut and sugar. Add the eggs and enough milk to make a soft, dropping consistency. Spoon into the prepared tin.

4. Bake in the oven for 1½ hours until well risen and springy to the touch.

5. Leave to cool in the tin for 5 minutes, then turn out to finish cooling on a wire rack.

Cornish Heavy Cake

✳ ✳ ✳ ✳ ✳ ✳ ✳ ✳

A traditional Cornish fruit cake, this is more akin to a pastry or a sweet bread than a cake – it is quite like a teacake or a hot cross bun in flavour and texture.

INGREDIENTS

Makes a 20×25cm/8×10in cake

350g/12oz plain flour, plus extra
   for dusting
a pinch of salt
175g/6oz lard or vegetable fat
75g/3oz caster sugar
175g/6oz currants
2 tbsp chopped mixed peel (optional)
2 tbsp milk
2 tbsp water
1 egg, beaten

METHOD

1. Heat the oven to 160°C/325°F/ gas 3 and grease and line a 20×25cm/8×10in baking tin.
2. Put the flour and salt in a bowl and rub in the lard until the mixture resembles coarse breadcrumbs, just like making pastry. Stir in the sugar, currants and mixed peel.

3. Mix together the milk and water and gradually add enough to mix to a soft dough. You may not need all the liquid.
4. Roll out to about 1cm/½in thick and place in the prepared baking tin. Brush with beaten egg, then draw a criss-cross pattern across the top with a knife.
5. Bake in the oven for about 20 minutes until golden. Leave to cool in the tin for 5 minutes, then turn out to finish cooling on a wire rack.

Fruited Cider Cake

✳ ✳ ✳ ✳ ✳ ✳ ✳ ✳

A moist cake, with the apple flavour of cider, this cake cuts well and also keeps well in airtight tin – so it is a good one to make if you just need a piece now and then.

INGREDIENTS

Makes an 18cm/7in cake
250g/9oz sultanas
150ml/5fl oz dry cider
100g/4oz butter
100g/4oz soft dark brown sugar
2 eggs
250g/9oz plain flour
1 tsp bicarbonate of soda

METHOD

1. Soak the sultanas in the cider overnight.
2. Heat the oven to 180°C/350°F/gas 4 and grease and line an 18cm/7in cake tin.
3. Beat together the butter and sugar until pale and creamy.
4. Gradually add the eggs, beating well, then blend in half the flour and the bicarbonate of soda. Stir in the soaked fruit with its liquid, then the remaining flour. Spoon into the prepared tin.
5. Bake in the oven for 30 minutes until springy to the touch.
6. Leave to cool in the tin for 5 minutes, then turn out to finish cooling on a wire rack.

Rhubarb & Honey Cake

❋ ❋ ❋ ❋ ❋ ❋ ❋ ❋

A soft-textured, dense cake, this could be served as a dessert with a generous dollop of crème fraîche, or as a cake in its own right. It is easiest to eat with a fork.

INGREDIENTS

Makes a 20×25cm/8×10in cake
225g/8oz clear honey
100ml3½fl oz sunflower oil
150g/5oz yogurt
1 egg
1 tsp vanilla extract
350g/12oz wholemeal flour
1 tbsp bicarbonate of soda
a pinch of salt
350g/12oz rhubarb, chopped

FOR THE TOPPING

75g/3oz muscovado sugar
1 tsp ground cinnamon
25g/1oz butter

METHOD

1. Heat the oven to 160°C/325°F/ gas 3 and grease and line a 20×25cm/8×10in cake tin.

2. Gently beat together the honey, oil, yogurt, egg and vanilla extract.

3. Mix in the flour, bicarbonate of soda and salt, then stir in the rhubarb. Spoon into the prepared tin.

4. Mix together the sugar and cinnamon for the topping and sprinkle over the top, then dot with the butter.

5. Bake in the oven for 1 hour until springy to the touch.

6. Leave to cool in the tin for 10 minutes, then turn out to finish cooling on a wire rack.

Pineapple Upside-down Cake

As the name suggests, this moist and delicious cake is baked with the topping on the base, then turned out to reveal the juicy pineapple on top.

INGREDIENTS

Makes a 20cm/8in cake

100g/4oz butter
100g/4oz soft light brown sugar
2 eggs, lightly beaten
2 tbsp reserved pineapple juice
100g/4oz plain flour
1 tsp baking powder

FOR THE TOPPING

400g/14oz canned pineapple rings in
   juice, drained and juice reserved
6 glacé cherries
75g/3oz butter
75g/3oz soft light brown sugar

METHOD

1. Heat the oven to 180°C/350°F/ gas 4 and grease and line a 20cm/8in cake tin.
2. Arrange the pineapple rings attractively on the base of the tin, cutting the rings if necessary. Dot with the cherries.
3. Melt together the butter and sugar for the topping, then pour it evenly over the pineapple.
4. To make the cake mixture, place the butter and sugar in a bowl and beat until pale and creamy. Gradually add the eggs and pineapple juice alternately with the flour and baking powder, and mix until you have a smooth batter. Spoon over the pineapple and level the surface.
5. Bake in the oven for 45 minutes until springy to the touch.
6. Leave to cool in the tin for 5 minutes, then invert on to a wire rack. Lift off the tin, then remove the lining paper, using a palette knife to press back any topping that sticks to the paper. Leave to finish cooling.

Apple Cake

❊ ❊ ❊ ❊ ❊ ❊ ❊ ❊

*Apple cake is a perennial favourite with many people because
it remains moist and soft, with the lovely flavour of apples.
You can use cooking apples, but add a little more sugar if you do so.*

INGREDIENTS

Makes a 20cm/8in cake
450g/1lb eating apples
2 tbsp lemon juice
100g/4oz butter
100g/4oz soft dark brown sugar
3 eggs
200g/7oz plain flour
1½ tsp baking powder
1 tsp ground cinnamon
½ tsp freshly grated nutmeg
25g/1oz demerara sugar

METHOD

1. Heat the oven to 180°C/350°F/
gas 4 and grease and line a
20cm/8in cake tin.
2. Peel and core the apples. Slice one
into rings and chop the remainder.
Toss with the lemon juice to prevent
discoloration.

3. Beat together the butter and
sugar until pale and creamy.
4. Add the eggs, flour, baking
powder, cinnamon and nutmeg
and mix until smooth. Stir in the
chopped apples and spoon into
the prepared cake tin. Arrange the
apple rings on top and sprinkle with
the demerara sugar.
5. Bake in the oven for 45 minutes
until well risen and golden brown.
6. Leave to cool in the tin for
5 minutes, then turn out to finish
cooling on a wire rack.

Pumpkin Cake

✳ ✳ ✳ ✳ ✳ ✳ ✳ ✳

Cans of pumpkin purée make this a really simple and delicious cake, although obviously you can use flesh from a pumpkin, boiled and puréed, if you prefer.

INGREDIENTS

Makes a 23cm/9in cake
400g/14oz can pumpkin purée
350g/12oz soft light brown sugar
100g/4oz butter
2 eggs
300g/11oz plain flour
2 tsp bicarbonate of soda
1 tbsp mixed spice

FOR THE FROSTING

100g/4oz butter
225g/8oz cream cheese
4 tbsp clear honey
a pinch of ground cloves

METHOD

1. Heat the oven to 180°C/350°F/ gas 4 and grease and line a 23cm/9in cake tin.
2. Beat the pumpkin, sugar, butter and eggs until well blended. Add the remaining cake ingredients and stir gently until combined. Spoon into the prepared tin.
3. Bake in the oven for 45 minutes until a skewer inserted in the centre comes out clean.
4. Leave to cool in the tin for 5 minutes, then turn out to finish cooling on a wire rack.
5. Beat all the frosting ingredients together. Spread on top of the cooled cake.

Carrot Cake with Cream Cheese Frosting

✳ ✳ ✳ ✳ ✳ ✳ ✳ ✳

Although we don't make many sweet treats with vegetables, they used to be quite common, carrot and beetroot being particularly popular.

INGREDIENTS

Makes a 20cm/8in cake

4 eggs, separated
225g/8oz butter
225g/8oz soft light brown sugar
finely grated zest of ½ orange
1 tbsp lemon juice
175g/6oz plain flour
100g/4oz walnuts, chopped
50g/2oz ground almonds
2 tsp baking powder
350g/12oz carrots, peeled and grated

FOR THE ICING

250g/9oz cream cheese
1 tbsp clear honey
1 tsp lemon juice

METHOD

1. Heat the oven to 180°C/350°F/ gas 4 and grease and line a 20cm/8in cake tin.

2. Beat the egg whites until stiff, then put to one side.

3. In a separate bowl, beat the butter and sugar until light and creamy.

4. Beat in the egg yolks, orange zest and lemon juice, followed by the flour, walnuts, ground almonds and baking powder. Fold in the carrots, then finally fold in the beaten egg whites using a metal spoon. Spoon into the prepared tin.

5. Bake in the oven for 1½ hours until firm and golden. Cover the top with baking paper if it starts to brown too quickly.

6. Leave to cool in the tin for 5 minutes, then turn out to finish cooling on to a wire rack.

7. To make the icing, beat the cheese, honey and lemon juice together and spread over the top of the cake.

Courgette Cake

✳ ✳ ✳ ✳ ✳ ✳ ✳ ✳

This is the perfect recipe for gardeners with a glut of courgettes.
Pick them while they are still small and tender and
they will make a cake with a lovely texture.

INGREDIENTS

Makes a 20cm/8in cake
250g/9oz plain flour
2 tsp ground cinnamon
1 tsp baking powder
1 tsp bicarbonate of soda
a pinch of salt
¼ tsp freshly grated nutmeg
100g/4oz soft light brown sugar
150ml/5fl oz sunflower oil
3 eggs, lightly beaten
1 tbsp golden syrup
1 tsp vanilla extract
250g/9oz courgettes, grated
50g/2oz chopped mixed nuts

FOR THE ICING

100g/4oz soft cream cheese
250g/9oz icing sugar, sifted

METHOD

1. Heat the oven to 180°C/350°F/ gas 4 and grease and line a 20cm/8in cake tin.

2. Mix the flour, cinnamon, baking powder, bicarbonate of soda, salt and half the nutmeg in a bowl. Stir in the sugar and make a well in the centre.

3. Add the oil, eggs, syrup and vanilla and beat until well blended. Fold in the courgettes and nuts. Spoon the mixture into the prepared tin.

4. Bake in the oven for 50 minutes until a skewer inserted in the centre comes out clean.

5. Leave to cool in the tin for 5 minutes, then turn out to finish cooling on a wire rack.

6. Beat together the icing ingredients with the remaining nutmeg and spread over the top.

Simple Carrot & Walnut Cake

✳ ✳ ✳ ✳ ✳ ✳ ✳ ✳

When you mix a cake that uses oil rather than butter the mixture may seem a little loose and look rather shiny, but it makes a super-moist cake.

INGREDIENTS

Makes a 20cm/8in cake
200ml/7fl oz sunflower oil
4 eggs
250ml/8fl oz clear honey
1 tsp vanilla extract
225g/8oz wholemeal flour
2 tsp baking powder
¼ tsp bicarbonate of soda
a pinch of salt
175g/6oz carrots, grated
175g/6oz sultanas
100g/4oz walnuts, chopped

METHOD

1. Heat the oven to 180°C/350°F/ gas 4 and grease and line a 20cm/8in cake tin.
2. In a bowl, mix the oil, eggs, honey and vanilla. Gradually beat in the flour, baking powder, bicarbonate of soda and salt. Fold in the carrots, sultanas and walnuts. Spoon into the prepared tin.
3. Bake in the oven for 1 hour until golden and springy to the touch.
4. Leave to cool in the tin for 5 minutes, then turn out to finish cooling on a wire rack.

Swedish Almond Cake

This cake cuts beautifully into neat slices. It has a lovely clean taste, with the subtle flavour of oranges added to the nutty texture of the almonds.

INGREDIENTS

Makes a 20cm/8in cake

4 eggs, separated
200g/7oz butter
200g/7oz caster sugar
200g/7oz self-raising flour
50g/2oz chopped almonds
grated zest of 1 orange
50g/2oz sultanas

METHOD

1. Heat the oven to 180°C/350°F/gas 4 and grease and line a 20cm/8in cake tin.

2. Whisk the egg whites until they form soft peaks.

3. In a separate bowl, beat together the butter and sugar until pale and creamy. Lightly beat the egg yolks, then beat into the mixture. Fold in the flour, almonds, orange zest and sultanas. Finally, fold in the beaten egg whites using a metal spoon, then spoon the mixture into the prepared tin.

4. Bake in the oven for 1 hour until well risen and golden brown. The cake should be springy to the touch.

5. Leave to cool in the tin for 5 minutes, then turn out to finish cooling on a wire rack.

COOK'S TIP

Always use a clean, grease-free bowl and whisk when whisking egg whites otherwise they will not stiffen. If you whisk them first, before all the other ingredients, then you can use your whisk for the other ingredients without having to wash it during preparation.

Hazelnut Cake

✳ ✳ ✳ ✳ ✳ ✳ ✳ ✳

Made with ground hazelnuts, this cake contains no flour so it is suitable for those who cannot tolerate gluten. The egg whites lift the cake and make it very light.

INGREDIENTS

Makes an 18cm/7in cake

100g/4oz hazelnuts

4 eggs, separated

150g/5oz caster sugar

FOR THE FILLING

50g/2oz butter

50g/2oz icing sugar, sifted

1 tbsp cocoa powder

1 tbsp instant coffee granules, rubbed through a sieve

METHOD

1. Heat the oven to 180°C/350°F/ gas 4 and grease and line two 18cm/7in cake tins.

2. Grind the hazelnuts finely in a food processor. Whisk the egg whites until stiff.

3. In a separate bowl, whisk the egg yolks with the sugar until pale and the mixture trails off the whisk in ribbons. Using a metal spoon, fold the nuts and egg whites alternately into the egg yolks. Spoon into the prepared tins.

4. Bake in the oven for 30 minutes until springy to the touch.

5. Leave to cool in the tin for 10 minutes, then turn out to finish cooling on a wire rack.

6. Blend the butter, icing sugar, cocoa and coffee to a smooth icing. Spread over one cake and place the other on top.

Coffee & Walnut Cake

✳ ✳ ✳ ✳ ✳ ✳ ✳ ✳

A particularly good combination of flavours makes this a stylish but simple cake. Make sure you cool the coffee before adding it to the cake mix.

INGREDIENTS

Makes a 20cm/8in cake
250g/9oz butter
250g/9oz soft light brown sugar
300g/11oz self-raising flour
2 tsp baking power
4 eggs
2 tbsp milk
2 tbsp strong black coffee, cooled
100g/4oz walnuts, chopped

FOR THE ICING
75g/3oz butter
200g/7oz icing sugar, sifted
1 tbsp ground walnuts
2 tsp coffee essence
a few walnut halves

METHOD

1. Heat the oven to 180°C/350°F/ gas 4 and grease and line a 20cm/8in cake tin.
2. Beat all the cake ingredients together until well blended. Spoon into the prepared tin.
3. Bake in the oven for 40 minutes until golden and springy to the touch. Leave to cool in the tin.
4. To make the icing, beat together the butter, icing sugar, ground walnuts and coffee essence, then spread over the top of the cake and decorate with walnut halves.

CHAPTER 7

* * * * * * * *

CHEESECAKES, TARTS & PASTRIES

This section concentrates on cheesecakes made with a creamy filling inside a shell, so you get the lovely contrast of flavours and textures between the outside – usually firm or crunchy – and the soft filling. Tarts are also baked in a sweet pastry shell – plus there are a few classic puff pastry favourites.

Sweet and cheesy

✳ ✳ ✳ ✳ ✳ ✳ ✳

There are two main kinds of cheesecake: whisked cheesecakes and baked cheesecakes. They have a shell to hold the ingredients together and provide a firm base, for which many use crushed biscuits pressed together with melted butter. You can choose different biscuits to give you a variety of textures and flavours, from digestives to ginger nuts. Biscuit bases can be baked or simply chilled – they work well either way. Some cheesecakes may also be baked using a sweet pastry base, providing you with yet more options.

Cream cheese is the basis of the soft filling. For whisked cheesecakes, it is mixed with gelatine so that, when chilled, it sets into a soft, mousse-like texture. A baked cheesecake includes eggs in the ingredients to set the mixture when it is baked in the oven.

Sweet tarts usually have a sweet pastry base, and a couple of firm favourites are included in this chapter. And, to finish, try your hand at some delectable continental pastries when you have a little extra time to spare in which to test your more advanced baking skills.

Whisked Surprise Cheesecake

✳ ✳ ✳ ✳ ✳ ✳ ✳ ✳

This is an unbaked cheesecake that uses gelatine to set the cream cheese filling, so it simply has to be assembled and chilled until you are ready to serve.

INGREDIENTS

Makes a 20cm/8in cheesecake

FOR THE BASE

100g/4oz butter, melted

250g/9oz digestive biscuits, crushed

FOR THE FILLING

1 banana, sliced

500g/1lb 2oz cream cheese

100g/4oz icing sugar, sifted

300ml/10fl oz double cream

400g/14oz strawberries

1 tbsp icing sugar, sifted

METHOD

1. Grease and line a 20cm/8in cake tin.

2. Melt the butter in a pan, then gradually stir in the crumbs, mixing all the time so the crumbs absorb the butter evenly. Press the crumb mixture over the base and up the sides of the prepared cake tin. Chill in the fridge while you make the filling.

3. Arrange the banana over the base.

4. Beat the cheese until soft, then beat in the icing sugar.

5. Whip the cream until stiff, then fold into the cheese mixture. Spoon over the banana base, making sure the bananas are covered. Chill overnight.

6. Slice or halve the strawberries and arrange on the top of the cheesecake, then sift a little icing sugar over the top.

CRUSHING BISCUITS

You can crush your biscuits in a food processor. Alternatively, put them in two bags, one inside the other, and crush them with a rolling pin. If you don't have a rolling pin, use a clean, empty bottle.

Lemon & Ginger Cheesecake

✳ ✳ ✳ ✳ ✳ ✳ ✳ ✳

Ginger is a very warming spice and makes a lovely contrast with the citrus tang of the filling. You could use any other type of biscuit if you don't have ginger.

INGREDIENTS

Makes a 20cm/8in cheesecake

FOR THE BASE
80g/3½oz butter
225g/8oz ginger biscuits, crushed
25g/1oz caster sugar
1 tsp ground cinnamon

FOR THE FILLING
2 eggs, separated
100g/4oz caster sugar
350g/12oz cream cheese
grated zest and juice of 1 lemon
150ml/5fl oz double cream

METHOD

1. Heat the oven to 160°C/325°F/ gas 3 and grease and line a 20cm/8in loose-based cake tin.
2. Melt the butter, then stir in the biscuit crumbs, sugar and cinnamon so that the crumbs absorb the butter evenly. Press the crumb mixture over the base and up the sides of the prepared cake tin. Chill in the fridge.
3. Whisk the egg whites until they hold soft peaks. Beat the egg yolks and sugar until thick and pale.
4. Beat the cheese until soft, then beat it into the egg mixture with the lemon zest and juice.
5. Whip the cream until it holds soft peaks when you lift out the whisk. Fold the cream into the cheese mixture, then fold in the egg whites using a metal spoon. Spoon the mixture into the base.
6. Bake in the oven for 1 hour until well risen and golden brown. The cheesecake may crack across the top. Turn off the oven but leave the cheesecake in the oven until it has cooled completely; it may sink. Chill before serving.

Layered Sultana Cheesecake

✾ ✾ ✾ ✾ ✾ ✾ ✾ ✾

Baked with layers of fruit and cheesecake between sweet pastry, this makes quite an unusual cheesecake, very attractive with its layer of sultanas.

INGREDIENTS

Makes a 20cm/8in square cake ❄

FOR THE BASE

175g/6oz butter
175g/6oz self-raising flour
50g/2oz cornflour
50g/2oz icing sugar, sifted
½ tsp freshly grated nutmeg

FOR THE FILLING

250g/9oz soft cheese
50g/2oz caster sugar
grated zest and juice of 1 lemon
3 eggs, separated
150ml/5fl oz double cream
75g/3oz sultanas

METHOD

1. Heat the oven to 200°C/400°F/ gas 6 and grease and line a 20cm/8in square cake tin.
2. Rub the butter into the flours until the mixture resembles breadcrumbs. Stir in the icing sugar and nutmeg.

Add 1 egg yolk from the eggs for the filling and mix to a soft pastry.
3. Roll out half the pastry on a floured surface and line the prepared tin. Prick with a fork, cover with baking paper, fill with baking beans and bake in the oven for 10 minutes.
4. Beat the cheese, sugar and lemon zest and juice until soft, then stir in the remaining egg yolks and the cream. Whisk the egg whites until stiff, then fold them in.
5. Remove the beans and paper from the base and reduce the oven temperature to 180°C/350°F/gas 4.
6. Sprinkle the base with sultanas, then spoon in the filling. Roll out the second half of the pastry and cut to fit the tin. Place gently on top.
7. Bake in the oven for 45 minutes until firm and golden.
8. Leave to cool in the tin, then cut into squares.

Caramel Swirl Cheesecake

✳ ✳ ✳ ✳ ✳ ✳ ✳ ✳

For this rich and delicious cheesecake swirled with caramel, you could also use ginger biscuits or hobnobs for the base.

INGREDIENTS

Makes a 20cm/8in cake

FOR THE BASE

50g/2oz butter

200g/7oz digestive biscuits, crushed

FOR THE FILLING

400g/14oz soft cheese

200ml/7fl oz crème fraîche

75g/3oz caster sugar

1 tbsp cornflour

3 eggs

1 tsp vanilla extract

400g/14oz can caramel

METHOD

1. Heat the oven to 180°C/350°F/ gas 4 and grease and line a 20cm/8in springform cake tin. Stand the cake tin in a large roasting tin.

2. Melt the butter in a pan, then gradually stir in the crumbs, mixing all the time so the crumbs absorb the butter evenly. Press into the base and

sides of the prepared tin and chill while you make the filling.

3. Beat the cheese, crème fraîche, sugar, cornflour, eggs and vanilla until thick and creamy.

4. Beat the caramel until smooth and pliable. Gently drizzle into the filling, then spoon over the base, so that the caramel remains marbled through the cheese. Pour boiling water into the roasting tin to come halfway up the sides of the cake tin.

5. Bake in the oven for 45 minutes, then turn off the oven but leave the cake in it, without opening the door, for 1 hour until both oven and cake are cool. Chill, preferably overnight, before serving.

Brandied Cheesecake Tarts

✳ ✳ ✳ ✳ ✳ ✳ ✳ ✳

This is my version of an old recipe that I believe comes from Yorkshire. If you are not fond of brandy, add a similar amount of orange juice or water.

INGREDIENTS *Makes 12*

FOR THE PASTRY

200g/7oz plain flour, plus extra
   for dusting
100g/4oz butter
50g/2oz caster sugar
1 egg yolk
2 tbsp water

FOR THE FILLING

175g/6oz curd cheese
40g/1½oz caster sugar
1 egg, separated
grated zest of 1 lemon
1 tbsp brandy
½ tsp freshly grated nutmeg
1 egg white
50g/2oz sultanas

METHOD

1. Heat the oven to 180°C/350°F/ gas 4 and grease a 12-hole cupcake tin. Put a large baking sheet in the oven to heat.

2. Put the flour and butter in a bowl and rub in the butter until the mixture resembles coarse breadcrumbs. Mix in the sugar.

3. Stir in the egg yolk and enough of the cold water to mix to a smooth dough.

4. Roll out the dough on a lightly floured surface and use to line the prepared tin.

5. Beat together the cheese, sugar, egg yolk, lemon zest, brandy and nutmeg until smooth. Whisk the 2 egg whites until stiff, then fold into the mixture using a metal spoon. Finally, fold in the sultanas. Spoon the mixture into the pastry cases and place the cupcake tin on the hot baking sheet.

6. Bake in the oven for 40 minutes until the filling is set and both pastry and filling are a light golden brown. Serve warm or cold.

Pear & Redcurrant Parcels

Make this in no time at all with ready-rolled pastry from the chiller cabinet. You can make your parcels whatever shape you find easiest.

INGREDIENTS *Makes 8 parcels* ❄️
375g/13oz pack ready-rolled
   puff pastry
flour, for dusting
2 ripe pears, peeled, cored
   and chopped
4 tbsp redcurrant jelly
1 egg, lightly beaten, or 2 tbsp milk
2 tbsp icing sugar, sifted

METHOD
1. Heat the oven to 200°C/400°F/ gas 6 and grease a baking sheet.
2. Lay out the pastry on a lightly floured surface and cut across into 8 strips. Roll each one out until it is about twice as wide as it started.
3. Mix the pears with the redcurrant jelly. Divide the mixture between the pastry strips, putting a spoonful almost at one end of each strip. Brush the edges with egg or milk. Fold one corner of the strip over

the filling to create a triangle shape, gently pressing the edge to seal. Then continue to fold the filling over, keeping the triangle shape, brushing with more egg or milk to seal the edges as you go.
4. Transfer to the baking sheet, brush with more egg or milk and sprinkle with half the icing sugar.
5. Bake in the oven for 15 minutes until puffy and golden.
6. Transfer to a wire rack to cool, then serve dusted with icing sugar.

Apple Strudel

*Originally an Austrian recipe, this is a classic pastry favourite.
Now you can buy filo pastry, instead of making your own, everyone
can have a go.*

INGREDIENTS *Makes 6*

700g/1½lb eating apples,
   peeled, cored and chopped
grated zest and juice of 1 orange
100g/4oz caster sugar
1 tsp freshly grated nutmeg
50g/2oz sultanas
8 sheets filo pastry
50g/2oz butter, melted
2 tbsp dried breadcrumbs

METHOD

1. Heat the oven to 190°C/375°F/
gas 5 and line a baking sheet.
2. Mix the apples, orange zest and
juice, sugar, nutmeg and sultanas.
3. Place one sheet of filo on the
prepared baking sheet and brush
with melted butter. Lay the next
sheet on top and brush with butter.
Continue in this way until you have
layered all the sheets.

4. Sprinkle with the breadcrumbs.
Spoon the filling down the centre of
the sheet. Fold one side of the pastry
over the filling, then use the baking
paper to help you roll up the pastry
like a Swiss roll. Turn seam-side
down on the baking sheet and brush
with the remaining butter.
5. Bake in the oven for 35 minutes
until puffy and golden brown. Cut
into 6 sections to serve.

Eccles Cakes

❋ ❋ ❋ ❋ ❋ ❋ ❋ ❋

These traditional English pastries are so easy to make with ready-made puff pastry, or you can make your own from scratch if you prefer.

INGREDIENTS *Makes 12*

225g/8oz currants
50g/2oz butter
50g/2oz soft dark brown sugar
450g/1lb puff pastry
a little flour, for dusting
1 egg, lightly beaten
25g/1oz demerara sugar

METHOD

1. Heat the oven to 200°C/400°F/ gas 6 and grease a large baking tray.
2. Put the currants, butter and sugar in a small saucepan over a low heat, stirring until melted. Remove from the heat and leave to cool.
3. You can roll out the pastry as one or two pieces then cut it, or cut it into 12 pieces first, then roll them out thinly. The underneath of the Eccles cake may be a bit uneven but nothing is wasted.
4. Roll out the pastry quite thinly on a lightly floured surface. Divide the filling between the pieces of pastry. Brush the edges of each one with a little egg, then fold in the sides and seal them together like a parcel, brushing with egg as necessary.
5. Turn them over and place seam-side down on the baking tray. Brush with egg, sprinkle with demerara sugar and cut 3 short slashes across the top of the pastry.
6. Bake in the oven for about 20 minutes until puffed up and golden, then transfer to a wire rack to cool.

Strawberry & Cream Mille Feuille

✳ ✳ ✳ ✳ ✳ ✳ ✳ ✳

So simple but so elegant, this is created from three layers of caramelized puff pastry separated by strawberries and whipped cream.

INGREDIENTS *Makes 4* ❄
500g/1lb 2oz puff pastry
flour, for dusting
50g/2oz icing sugar, sifted
300ml/10fl oz double or
   whipping cream
400g/14oz strawberries,
   halved if large

METHOD
1. Heat the oven to 200°C/400°F/
gas 6 and grease 2 or 3 large
baking sheets.
2. Roll out the pastry on a lightly
floured surface and trim into six
15×20cm/6×8in rectangles. Place on
the baking sheets and sprinkle with
half the icing sugar.
3. Bake in the oven for 10 minutes.
Remove from the oven and split each
piece horizontally. Arrange cut-sides
up on the baking sheets and sprinkle
with most of the remaining sugar.

Return to the oven for a further
10 minutes until the pastry is cooked
through and golden. Remove from
the oven and transfer to wire racks
to cool.
4. While the pastry is cooling, whip
the cream until stiff.
5. To assemble the cakes, choose
the best slices to keep for the top.
Place 4 slices on a serving plate and
top with half the strawberries and
half the cream. Place another pastry
slice on each one and cover with the
remaining strawberries and cream.
Top with the final slice and sprinkle
with icing sugar to serve.

Apple Danish Pastries

✳ ✳ ✳ ✳ ✳ ✳ ✳ ✳

*These are not for the faint-hearted – they take a while to make,
so allow plenty of time. They are best eaten on the day they are
made and are not suitable for freezing.*

INGREDIENTS *Makes 12*

FOR THE DOUGH
450g/1lb strong plain flour,
   plus extra for dusting
a pinch of salt
350g/12oz butter, softened
50g/2oz caster sugar
1 sachet easy-blend dried yeast
150ml/5fl oz warm milk, plus a
   little extra milk for sealing
2 eggs, lightly beaten

FOR THE FILLING
450g/1lb cooking apples,
   quartered and cored
grated zest and juice of 1 lemon
15g/½oz butter
75g/3oz soft light brown sugar

FOR THE ICING
75g/3oz icing sugar, sifted
1 tbsp hot water

METHOD
1. Put the flour and salt in a bowl
and rub in 50g/2oz of the butter
until the mixture resembles coarse
breadcrumbs. Mix in the sugar
and yeast.

2. Stir in the milk and eggs and mix
to a smooth dough. Put in a clean
bowl, cover with oiled clingfilm and
leave in a warm place for about
1 hour until doubled in size.

3. Meanwhile, make the filling. Put
the apples, lemon zest and juice and
butter in a pan, bring to the boil,
then reduce the heat, cover and
simmer gently for about 15 minutes
until soft. Rub through a sieve, then
return to the pan, add the sugar and
simmer gently for about 5 minutes
until thick. Leave to cool.

4. Knead the pastry again until smooth, then roll out on a lightly floured surface to about 33×23cm/13×9in. Dot the top two-thirds of the dough with half the remaining butter. Fold up the bottom one-third, then fold down the top third. Turn the pastry 90 degrees so the fold is on the left, and repeat the rolling, buttering and folding, which will use up the butter. Wrap in clingfilm and put in the fridge for 20 minutes.

5. With the fold on the left, roll out and fold the dough, as before but without the butter, twice more. Wrap and chill as before.

6. Grease 2 baking sheets. Cut the dough in half and roll out one half to 20×30cm/8×12in and cut into 10cm/4in squares. Divide half the filling between the squares, then fold the corners into the middle, sealing with a little milk. Place on the baking sheets. Repeat with the other half. Cover with oiled clingfilm and leave in a warm place for 15 minutes until beginning to rise.

7. Heat the oven to 220°C/425°F/ gas 7. Uncover the pastries, brush with a little milk and bake in the oven for 15 minutes until puffy and golden brown.

8. Transfer the pastries to a wire rack with a sheet of kitchen paper underneath the rack. Put the icing sugar in a small bowl and gradually mix in the water until smooth. Drizzle in lines over the warm pastries, then leave to cool.

Almond Slices

✳ ✳ ✳ ✳ ✳ ✳ ✳ ✳

This is a classic and delicious almond dish – you are bound to enjoy the luscious layer of pastry spread with your favourite jam and topped with a light mixture made with ground almonds.

INGREDIENTS *Makes 12*

FOR THE PASTRY
225g/8oz plain flour, plus extra
   for dusting
100g/4oz butter
50g/2oz caster sugar
1 egg yolk
1–2 tbsp milk (optional)
100g/4oz raspberry jam

FOR THE FILLING
100g/4oz plain flour
100g/4oz ground almonds
200g/7oz butter
200g/7oz caster sugar
2 tsp baking powder
1 tsp almond extract
3 eggs
100g/4oz flaked almonds

METHOD

1. Grease and line a 20×30cm/ 8×12in Swiss roll tin.
2. Put the flour in a bowl and rub in the butter until the mixture resembles coarse breadcrumbs. Stir in the sugar. Add the egg yolk and mix to a soft dough, with a little of the milk, if necessary.
3. Roll out on a lightly floured surface and press gently to fit the prepared tin, shaping the edges to create a border. Chill for 15 minutes.
4. Heat the oven to 200°C/400°F/ gas 6.
5. Prick the base of the pastry case all over with a fork and bake in the oven for 10 minutes until just cooked.

6. Meanwhile, beat together all the filling ingredients except the flaked almonds until smooth.

7. Spread the jam over the pastry, then spoon the filling over the top and sprinkle with the almonds.

8. Reduce the oven temperature to 180°C/350°F/gas 4 and bake for about 40 minutes until well risen and golden brown.

9. Leave to cool in the tin for 5 minutes, then turn out on to a wire rack to finish cooling. Cut into bars to serve.

LIFTING PASTRY

When you have rolled out pastry to line a baking tin, the way to lift it is to gently turn one side over your rolling pin and lift it over the tin, placing it down gently.

Baklava

✴ ✴ ✴ ✴ ✴ ✴ ✴ ✴

This almond pastry drenched with flavoured syrup is popular throughout Greece, Turkey and the Middle East and is served as a special treat.

INGREDIENTS *Makes 12 pastries*

225g/8oz caster sugar
150ml/5fl oz water
1 tbsp lemon juice
1 tbsp orange juice
275g/10oz filo pastry sheets
  (6 sheets), cut in half
75g/3oz butter, melted
100g/4oz ground almonds
50g/2oz chopped almonds

METHOD

1. Stir the sugar, water and juices in a pan over a gentle heat until dissolved, then raise the heat and simmer for about 5 minutes until thick enough to coat the back of a spoon. Leave to cool, then chill.
2. Heat the oven to 160°C/325°F/gas 3 and grease a large roasting tin.
3. Place a sheet of filo pastry in the tin and brush with melted butter. Place another sheet on top and brush with butter. Repeat with 2 more sheets. Sprinkle with half the ground almonds and half the chopped almonds, then spoon 5 tbsp of the syrup over.
4. Layer the next 4 sheets of the pastry, brushing with butter as before, then top with the remaining ground and chopped almonds and another 5 tbsp of the syrup. Finish with the remaining pastry sheets, brushing the top sheet with melted butter. Use a sharp serrated knife to cut the baklava into diamond shapes.
5. Bake in the oven for 25 minutes. Increase the oven temperature to 220°C/425°/gas 7 and bake for a further 15 minutes until golden and crisp round the edges.
6. Pour the remaining cold syrup over the hot pastry and leave to cool. Cut into diamond shapes when cold. Trim off the crunchy edges if preferred.

CHAPTER 8

❋❋❋❋❋❋❋❋

TEABREADS & YEAST BAKING

Now you can enjoy some substantial yeasted cakes and other baked goodies that could be defined as either a cake or a fancy bread. Whatever you call them, they taste delicious sliced and topped with fresh unsalted butter.

Whichever way you slice it

✳ ✳ ✳ ✳ ✳ ✳ ✳

Teabreads may get their name from the fruit being soaked in tea before being mixed into the cake. Equally, it may be because they are served at tea time.

I like to make many of these rich and dense teabreads in a loaf tin. It not only seems appropriate, it is also extremely convenient to pop a loaf-tin liner in a tin, spoon in the mixture and put it in the oven. It might be a bit lazy, but ready-made paper loaf-tin liners are a quick and easy option. Flexible silicone loaf 'tins' are also very easy to use and avoid any of the problems of cake mixtures sticking to the tins – disappointing when it happens and so easily avoided.

Having the teabread in a loaf shape also makes them easier to slice, and that's the best way to serve them – sliced and buttered, accompanied by a hot cup of tea.

SOAKING THE FRUIT
If you soak your fruit, the raisins, currants or sultanas absorb the liquid and plump up, retaining all that lovely moisture to enhance the texture and flavour of the teabread.

Traditional Teabread

✻ ✻ ✻ ✻ ✻ ✻ ✻ ✻

There are many regional versions of teabreads, but all share the theme of lots of dried fruit mix, and they all taste great spread with butter.

INGREDIENTS

Makes a 900g/2lb teabread
150g/5oz soft dark brown sugar
150g/5oz sultanas
150g/5oz stoned dates, chopped
300ml/10fl oz black tea
2 tbsp whisky
250g/9oz plain flour
1 egg, lightly beaten
2 tsp baking powder
1½ tsp mixed spice
2 tbsp honey, warmed

METHOD

1. Heat the oven to 150°C/300°F/ gas 3 and grease and line a 900g/2lb loaf tin.
2. Soak the sugar and fruit in the tea and whisky overnight.
3. Gradually add the remaining ingredients except the honey and mix until well blended. Spoon the mixture into the prepared tin.
4. Bake in the oven for about 1½ hours until well risen, dark golden and firm to the touch.
5. Leave to cool in the tin for 5 minutes, then turn out on to a wire rack.
6. Brush the top with the honey, then leave to finish cooling.

Honeyed Teabread

✳ ✳ ✳ ✳ ✳ ✳ ✳ ✳

Firm and slightly nutty, this is flavoured with coffee and orange, making it a somewhat sophisticated version of the traditional teabread.

INGREDIENTS

Makes a 900g/2lb teabread
3 eggs
150g/5oz soft dark brown sugar
300g/11oz clear honey
40g/1½oz butter, melted
2 tbsp instant coffee
150ml/5fl oz hot water
300g/11oz plain flour
2 tsp ground cinnamon
1 tsp baking powder
½ tsp bicarbonate of soda
½ tsp salt
100g/4oz walnuts, chopped
grated zest of 1 orange

METHOD

1. Heat the oven to 180°C/350°F/ gas 4 and grease and line a 900g/2lb loaf tin.
2. Beat together the eggs and sugar until blended, then beat in the honey and melted butter.
3. Dissolve the coffee in the water. Mix the flour, cinnamon, baking powder, bicarbonate of soda and salt. Take 2 tbsp of the mixture and toss with the walnuts to coat.
4. Add the flour mixture to the egg mixture a little at a time, alternating with the coffee. Fold in the walnuts and orange zest. Spoon into the prepared tin.
5. Bake in the oven for 1 hour until well risen and firm.
6. Leave to cool in the tin. Wrap in foil and store for at least 2 days before serving.

Apricot, Prune & Maple Syrup Teabread

The great thing about teabreads is that they are beautifully moist. If you are not that keen on prunes, don't worry – they add a lovely texture and only a very subtle flavour.

INGREDIENTS

Makes a 900g/2lb teabread

100g/4oz ready-to-eat dried apricots, chopped
50g/2oz prunes, chopped
200g/7oz plain flour
100g/4oz soft dark brown sugar
2 tsp baking powder
2 tsp ground cinnamon
100ml/4fl oz maple syrup
200ml/7fl oz milk
1 egg, lightly beaten

METHOD

1. Heat the oven to 180°C/350°F/ gas 4 and grease and line a 900g/2lb loaf tin.
2. Toss the apricots and prunes in a little of the flour.
3. Mix the rest of the flour with the sugar, baking powder and cinnamon. Gradually mix in the maple syrup, milk and egg, then fold in the fruit. Spoon into the prepared tin.
4. Bake in the oven for 45 minutes until well risen, dark golden brown and fairly firm to the touch.
5. Leave to cool in the tin for 5 minutes, then turn out on to a wire rack to finish cooling.

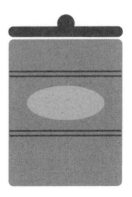

Banana & Raisin Cake

Banana cakes have quite a dense, moist texture, and can be served either on their own or sliced and given a layer of butter for extra deliciousness.

INGREDIENTS

Makes a 900g/2lb loaf cake

100g/4oz wholemeal flour
100g/4oz soft dark brown sugar
50g/2oz chopped mixed nuts
100g/4oz rolled oats
100g/4oz raisins
1 egg, lightly beaten
120ml/4fl oz sunflower oil
½ tsp almond extract
4 bananas, mashed

METHOD

1. Heat the oven to 180°C/350°F/gas 4 and grease and line a 900g/2lb loaf tin.

2. Mix together all the ingredients in a large bowl until soft and well blended. Spoon into the prepared tin.

3. Bake in the oven for 45 minutes until well risen and firm to the touch. A skewer inserted in the centre should come out clean.

4. Leave to cool in the tin for 5 minutes, then turn out on to a wire rack to finish cooling.

VARIATIONS

Use sultanas, chopped dried apricots, dried cranberries or even mixed fruit instead of the raisins.

Italian Pasta, Almond & Date Loaf

❋ ❋ ❋ ❋ ❋ ❋ ❋ ❋

The idea of pasta in a cake is unusual, but it gives the cake a pleasingly dense texture, not unlike a bread pudding. It is also a great way to use up leftover pasta.

INGREDIENTS

Makes a 20cm/8in loaf cake
150g/5oz cooked pasta
100g/4oz plain flour
2 tsp baking powder
½ tsp ground cinnamon
75g/3oz butter
50g/2oz caster sugar
25g/1oz flaked almonds
100g/4oz dates, stoned
3 eggs

METHOD

1. Heat the oven to 200°C/400°F/ gas 6 and grease and line a 900g/2lb loaf tin.

2. Put the pasta in a food processor and chop roughly. Add all the remaining ingredients and process until well blended. Spoon into the prepared tin.

3. Bake in the oven for about 30 minutes until well risen and golden on top. A skewer inserted into the centre should come out clean.

4. Leave to cool in the tin for 5 minutes, then turn out on to a wire rack to finish cooling.

German Friendship Cake

The idea of a friendship cake is that the sourdough starter is passed round a circle of friends – hence the name.

INGREDIENTS

Makes a 20×25cm/8×10in cake

FOR THE STARTER

120ml/4fl oz sourdough starter (right)
120ml/4fl oz milk
100g/4oz caster sugar
50g/2oz plain flour

FOR THE CAKE

200ml/7fl oz sunflower oil
250g/9oz soft light brown sugar
3 eggs, lightly beaten
2 tsp vanilla extract
200g/7oz plain flour
2 tsp baking powder
1½ tsp bicarbonate of soda
2 tsp ground cinnamon
½ tsp freshly grated nutmeg
a pinch of ground cloves

SOURDOUGH STARTER

Sourdough starters use natural yeasts to create a bubbly mixture that you can keep feeding and using. To begin, blend a cup of milk (200ml/7fl oz) with a cup of plain flour (100g/4oz) and a cup of caster sugar (225g/8oz), cover with clingfilm and leave at room temperature for 4 days, stirring daily. On the fifth day, stir in another cup each of flour, milk and sugar. Stir daily for the following 4 days, then stir in a cup each of flour, milk and sugar on the tenth day and stir well. Traditionally, you then use one quarter to bake a cake and give away the remainder to your friends, who keep it alive and pass it on.

METHOD

1. Mix the starter with the milk, sugar and flour. Cover with clingfilm and leave in a warm place for 24 hours.

2. Heat the oven to 180°C/350°F/ gas 4 and grease and line a 20×25cm/8×10in cake tin.

3. Beat together the oil, sugar, eggs and vanilla until pale. Beat in the starter.

4. Stir the dry ingredients together, then blend them into the egg mixture. Spoon into the prepared tin.

5. Bake in the oven for 40 minutes until well risen and firm to the touch.

6. Leave to cool in the tin for 5 minutes, then turn out to finish cooling on a wire rack.

Crunchy-topped Banana Bread

✳ ✳ ✳ ✳ ✳ ✳ ✳ ✳

There's a fine line between a teabread and a cake, and this moist cake sits right on the line. You can serve it sliced and buttered or just on its own.

INGREDIENTS

Makes a 900g/2lb loaf cake
100g/4oz butter
100g/4oz soft dark brown sugar
2 eggs
150g/5 oz plain flour
1 tsp baking powder
1 tsp bicarbonate of soda
1½ tsp ground cinnamon
75ml/2½fl oz milk
2 bananas, mashed

FOR THE TOPPING

25g/1oz butter
25g/1oz demerara sugar
50g/2oz crunchy clusters cereal
½ tsp ground cinnamon

METHOD

1. Heat the oven to 180°C/350°F/
gas 4 and grease and line a
900g/2lb loaf tin.
2. Beat together the butter and
sugar until light and creamy.
Gradually beat in the remaining cake
ingredients, folding in the bananas
last. Spoon into the prepared tin.
3. For the topping, melt the butter
and demerara sugar in a small pan,
then stir in the cereal and cinnamon.
Spoon over the top of the cake.
4. Bake in the oven for 30 minutes
until well risen and crunchy on top.
A skewer inserted in the centre
should come out clean.
5. Leave to cool in the tin for
5 minutes, then turn out to finish
cooling on a wire rack.

Panettone

This Italian fruited yeast cake is traditionally eaten at Christmas and New Year. However, it is a welcome treat at any season and is delicious either fresh or toasted and spread with butter.

INGREDIENTS

Makes a 20cm/8in cake

350g/12oz plain flour
a pinch of salt
2 tsp fast-action dried yeast
50g/2oz caster sugar
50g/2oz sultanas
50g/2oz hazelnuts, roughly chopped
finely grated zest of 1 orange
3 eggs, lightly beaten
125g/4½oz butter, softened
75ml/2½fl oz warm milk
15g/½oz icing sugar, sifted

METHOD

1. Grease and line a 20cm/8in panettone tin or fluted brioche tin.
2. Mix together the flour, salt, yeast, sugar, sultanas, hazelnuts and orange zest.

3. Mix in the eggs, butter and enough milk to mix to a firm dough. Knead until all the ingredients come together, then keep kneading for about 5 minutes until the dough is smooth, elastic and no longer sticky. Put in an oiled bowl, cover with oiled clingfilm and leave in a warm place for about 1½ hours until doubled in size.
4. Knock the dough back, then put it in the prepared tin, cover and leave to rise again.
5. Heat the oven to 180°C/350°F/ gas 4.
6. Bake the panettone in the oven for 30 minutes until well risen.
7. Remove from the oven, cover with a clean tea towel and leave to cool. Remove from the tin and dust with icing sugar to serve.

Saffron Cake

❊ ❊ ❊ ❊ ❊ ❊ ❊ ❊

Saffron is the dried stigmas of the autumn crocus (Crocus sativus), which have to be harvested by hand, three per flower. Not surprisingly, it is the most expensive spice in the world.

INGREDIENTS

Makes a 20cm/8in cake
150ml/5fl oz boiling water
a pinch of saffron strands
450g/1lb strong plain flour
a pinch of salt
1 tbsp fast-action dried yeast
50g/2oz caster sugar
100g/4oz butter
175g/6oz currants
grated zest of 1 lemon
150ml/5fl oz milk

METHOD

1. Pour the boiling water over the saffron strands and leave to soak overnight.
2. Grease and line a 20cm/8in cake tin.
3. In a bowl, mix the flour, salt, yeast and sugar. Rub in the butter until the mixture resembles coarse breadcrumbs. Stir in the currants and lemon zest.
4. Warm the milk until lukewarm; if you put your finger in it you should be able to feel it as neither hot nor cold. Mix into the flour, then strain in the saffron liquid. Beat the mixture thoroughly, then turn into the prepared tin, cover with oiled clingfilm and leave in a warm place to rise for about 1 hour. It should almost fill the tin.
5. Meanwhile heat the oven to 200°C/400°F/gas 6.
6. Bake in the oven for 30 minutes. Reduce the oven temperature to 180°C/350°F/gas 4 and bake for a further 30 minutes without opening the oven door.
7. Leave to cool in the tin for 5 minutes, then turn out to finish cooling on a wire rack.

CHAPTER 9

GLUTEN-FREE CAKES & MERINGUES

This section offers gluten-free recipes and also sets down some principles so that those who are intolerant to gluten will be able to adapt some of their own recipes and join in on special-occasion cakes.

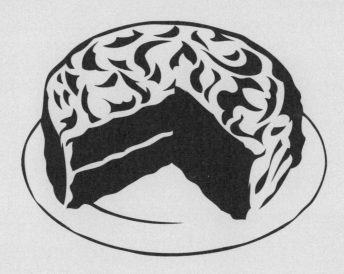

Making gluten-free cakes

❋ ❋ ❋ ❋ ❋ ❋ ❋

These recipes are bound to be a hit with family and friends, whether or not they have a problem with gluten.

A protein in wheat and other cereals, gluten gives bread and cakes their elasticity, making them soft and chewy. Without it, baking bread or cakes is not successful because everything can go flat and hard. So if we cannot use traditional cereals we need to find alternative ingredients that can bring the spring back into baking.

You have probably already learnt what you need to avoid, but if this is a recent problem or you are baking for a gluten-intolerant guest, go through your food cupboard and read the labels. Here are a few things to look out for – but this is not an exhaustive list, so do check products before buying.

❋ Wheat flours of all kinds and anything made with them, so bread, cakes, pasta, and cereals.

❋ Any wheat products such as wheatgerm, semolina, couscous or bran.

❋ Products containing rye, barley, spelt and kamut. Some people who are gluten-intolerant also cannot tolerate oats, which contain a protein similar to gluten and may have been milled in equipment used for wheat, rye and barley.

❋ Raising agents such as baking powder.

❋ Spices, which sometimes use wheat flour to stop them clumping.

❋ Sauces, condiments or anything that is thickened with wheat flour.

Don't dwell on what you can't eat – be imaginative and find things you can, and ways of adapting your favourite recipes. Special gluten-free flours, baking powder and other products are readily available, including xanthan gum, a natural product that will restore the moist, springy texture that you lose when you bake without gluten.

Gluten-free Treacle & Ginger Muffins

✳ ✳ ✳ ✳ ✳ ✳ ✳ ✳

Rich and dark, these are deliciously gooey muffins. Don't keep them just for your gluten-intolerant friends – everyone can enjoy them.

INGREDIENTS *Makes 12*

225g/8oz plain gluten-free flour
2 tsp gluten-free baking powder
1 tsp xanthan gum
1 tsp ground ginger
100g/4oz black treacle
120ml/4fl oz sunflower oil
250ml/8fl oz milk
1 egg, lightly beaten

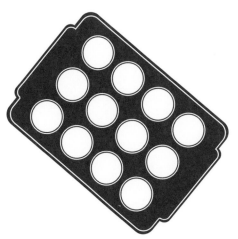

METHOD

1. Heat the oven to 200°C/400°F/ gas 6 and line a 12-hole muffin tin with paper cases.

2. Mix together the flour, baking powder, xanthan gum and ginger.

3. Measure the treacle, oil and milk into a measuring jug and add the egg. Pour into the dry ingredients and mix quickly to a slightly gluey batter. Spoon into the prepared muffin cases.

4. Bake in the oven for 20 minutes until well risen and springy to the touch. Transfer to a wire rack to cool.

Gluten-free Vanilla Muffins

These are light and delicious for any occasion. When you have used a vanilla pod, leave the pod in a jar of sugar to flavour it for another time.

INGREDIENTS *Makes 12*

225g/8oz plain gluten-free flour
2 tsp gluten-free baking powder
1 tsp xanthan gum
100g/4oz vanilla sugar or caster sugar
1 vanilla pod or 1 tsp vanilla extract
120ml/4fl oz sunflower oil
250ml/8fl oz milk
1 egg, lightly beaten

METHOD

1. Heat the oven to 200°C/400°F/gas 6 and line a 12-hole muffin tin with paper cases.

2. Mix together the flour, baking powder, xanthan gum and sugar. Split the vanilla pod, if using, and scrape the seeds into the bowl.

3. Measure the oil and milk into a measuring jug and add the egg. Add the vanilla extract, if using. Pour into the dry ingredients and mix quickly to a slightly gluey batter. Spoon into the prepared muffin cases.

4. Bake in the oven for 20 minutes until well risen and springy to the touch. Transfer to a wire rack to cool.

Gluten-free Cranberry & Nut Cake

✳ ✳ ✳ ✳ ✳ ✳ ✳ ✳

Cranberries contribute lovely dark red fruit amidst the moist and delicious cake. You can use light brown or caster sugar if you prefer.

INGREDIENTS

Makes a 900g/2lb loaf cake
150g/5oz sultanas
100g/4oz soft dark brown sugar
250ml/8fl oz hot black tea
125g/4½oz gluten-free plain flour
2 tsp gluten-free baking powder
1 tsp xanthan gum
1 tsp ground cinnamon
100g/4oz butter
50g/2oz chopped mixed nuts
50g/2oz dried cranberries

METHOD

1. Soak the sultanas and sugar in the hot tea, preferably overnight.
2. Heat the oven to 180°C/350°F/gas 4 and grease and line a 20cm/8in loaf tin.
3. Beat together the flour, baking powder, xanthan gum, ground cinnamon and butter, then mix in the sultanas and liquid with the nuts and cranberries. Spoon into the prepared tin.
4. Bake in the oven for about 40 minutes until well risen and springy to the touch.
5. Leave to cool in the tin for 5 minutes, then turn out on to a wire rack to finish cooling.

Gluten-free Hazelnut Milk Cake

❊ ❊ ❊ ❊ ❊ ❊ ❊ ❊

*This is based on the classic Mexican très leches cake, or 'three milk' cake.
Use the leftover milks instead of milk in any recipe.*

INGREDIENTS

Makes a 20×25cm/8×10in cake
100g/4oz gluten-free plain flour
1½ tsp gluten-free baking powder
1 tsp xanthan gum
a pinch of salt
5 eggs, separated
225g/8oz caster sugar
75ml/2½fl oz milk
1 tsp vanilla extract
400g/14oz can sweetened
  condensed milk
400g/14oz can evaporated milk
60ml/2fl oz double cream

METHOD

1. Heat the oven to 180°C/350°F/
gas 4. Grease and line a
20×25cm/8×10in baking tin.
2. Mix the flour, baking powder,
xanthan gum and salt in a large bowl.
3. Beat the egg yolks with 175g/6oz
of the sugar until pale and doubled in
volume. Add the milk and vanilla and
stir together very gently. Gently stir
the egg yolk mixture into the flour.
4. Beat the egg whites until they form
soft peaks. Still beating, pour in the
remaining sugar and continue to beat
until the whites are stiff but not dry.
Use a metal spoon to fold the egg
whites into the cake mixture, then
spoon the mixture into the prepared
pan and level the top.
5. Bake in the oven for 40 minutes until
risen and spongy.
6. Turn out into a deep dish and
leave to cool completely.
7. Mix the condensed milk, evaporated
milk and cream in a jug, then remove
300ml/½pt which you will not need.
8. Prick the cake all over with a fork.
Slowly spoon the milk evenly over
the cake. Leave to stand for about
30 minutes before serving so the
milk mixture is absorbed.

Gluten-free Teabread

❊ ❊ ❊ ❊ ❊ ❊ ❊ ❊

*You shouldn't have to miss out on tea-time treats just because
of a food intolerance, so here's a lovely fruity teabread.*

INGREDIENTS

Makes a 900g/2lb loaf cake
250g/9oz sultanas
250g/9oz raisins
175g/6oz soft light brown sugar
250ml/8fl oz strong black tea
1 egg, lightly beaten
250g/9oz gluten-free plain flour
1 tsp ground cinnamon
½ tsp bicarbonate of soda
½ tsp xanthan gum

METHOD

1. Soak the sultanas, raisins and
sugar in the tea overnight.

2. Heat the oven to 180°C/350°F/
gas 4 and grease and line a
900g/2lb loaf tin.
3. Mix the egg into the fruit and
tea mixture, then add the flour,
cinnamon, bicarbonate of soda and
xanthan gum. Blend thoroughly.
Spoon into the prepared loaf tin.
4. Bake in the oven for 1½ hours
until well risen and firm. Cover the
top with foil or baking paper if it
appears to be browning too quickly.
5. Leave to cool in the tin for
5 minutes, then turn out on to a
wire rack to finish cooling.

Gluten-free Polenta Cake

❋ ❋ ❋ ❋ ❋ ❋ ❋ ❋

This makes a lovely moist cake that combines polenta, ground almonds and a little gluten-free flour to replace the wheat flour.

INGREDIENTS

Makes a 23cm/9in cake
350g/12oz butter
300g/11oz caster sugar
4 eggs
125g/4½oz polenta
300g/11oz ground almonds
2 tbsp gluten-free plain flour
1½ tsp gluten-free baking powder
grated zest and juice of 2 lemons

FOR THE SYRUP
100g/4oz caster sugar
juice of 1 lemon

FOR THE ICING
250g/9oz mascarpone
50g/2oz icing sugar, sifted
grated zest of 1 lemon
20g/¾oz flaked almonds

METHOD

1. Heat the oven to 160°C/325°F/ gas 3 and grease and line a 23cm/9in springform cake tin.
2. Beat together the butter and sugar until pale and creamy. Gradually beat in the eggs, one at a time, then fold in the polenta, ground almonds, flour and baking powder. Fold in the lemon zest and juice. Spoon the mixture into the prepared tin.
3. Bake in the oven for 1 hour until a skewer inserted in the centre comes out clean. Cover with foil if the top appears to be browning too much.
4. While the cake is cooking, put the sugar and lemon juice in a pan over

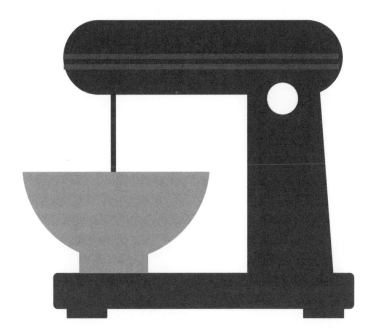

a low heat until the sugar is melted. Boil for a few minutes, without stirring, to create a golden syrup. Remove from the heat.

5. Remove the cake from the oven and prick the top with a skewer. Spoon the syrup over, then leave to cool in the tin for 20 minutes. Turn out to finish cooling on a wire rack.

6. Beat the mascarpone with the icing sugar and lemon zest until creamy. Spread on top of the cake and sprinkle with the almonds.

SPRINGFORM TINS

Springform tins make it easier to remove a cake, especially if it has a soft centre, as you can unclip the sides to lift them away from the cake. Loose-based tins are also handy. Sit the cake on a bowl that is smaller in diameter but taller than the cake tin and slide the sides down off the cake.

Hazelnut Meringues

✳ ✳ ✳ ✳ ✳ ✳ ✳ ✳

This recipe makes 12 cute, nutty little meringues. The hazelnuts give them a slightly more robust flavour than a traditional meringue made with just sugar.

INGREDIENTS *Makes 12*
100g/4oz hazelnuts
2 egg whites
100g/4oz caster sugar
a few drops of vanilla extract

METHOD
1. Heat the oven to 120°C/250°F/ gas ½. Grease and line a baking sheet.
2. Reserve 12 nuts for decoration. Finely chop or crush the remainder.
3. Whisk the egg whites until stiff. Gradually whisk in half the sugar until the mixture is very stiff and shiny. Add the crushed hazelnuts and the vanilla and keep whisking while you add the remaining sugar.
4. Spoon or pipe rounds of the meringue on to the baking sheet and top each one with a hazelnut.
5. Bake in the oven for 3 hours until crisp. Transfer to a wire rack to cool.

A CHOICE OF NUTS
You can use either finely chopped or crushed nuts for your meringues.

Gluten-free Almond Meringue Gâteau

A splendid layered cake, this is perfect for a special occasion as it looks very attractive with a buttercream topping finished with flaked nuts.

INGREDIENTS

Makes a 23cm/9in cake

75g/3oz flaked almonds
6 egg whites
300g/11oz caster sugar
3 tbsp ground almonds
15g/½oz cornflour
1 quantity Coffee Buttercream (page 152)
15g/½oz icing sugar, sifted

METHOD

1. Toast the almonds in a dry pan until golden. Tip on to a plate and leave to cool.

2. Heat the oven to 120°C/250°F/gas ½ and grease and line 2 large baking sheets. Draw three 23cm/9in circles on the paper by drawing round the base of a plate or cake tin.

3. Whisk the egg whites until stiff. Gradually whisk in half the sugar until the mixture holds stiff peaks, then add the ground almonds and cornflour and continue to whisk in the sugar until firm and glossy.

4. Spoon the meringue into a piping bag and pipe 3 closed spirals of meringue on to the paper.

5. Bake in the oven for 1 hour until dry, then turn on to a wire rack to cool.

6. Make the buttercream. Place the first meringue on a plate, spread with one-quarter of the buttercream, then top with the next meringue, more buttercream and the final meringue. Spread the remaining buttercream over the sides, or the top and sides, if you prefer. Press the toasted almonds into the icing on the sides of the cake. Dust the top with icing sugar to finish.

Strawberry Meringue Baskets

✳ ✳ ✳ ✳ ✳ ✳ ✳ ✳

You can make the meringues in advance, but do not assemble the baskets until just before serving otherwise they will go soft.

INGREDIENTS *Makes 8 meringues*
4 egg whites, at room temperature
200g/7oz caster sugar
1 tsp vanilla extract
250ml/8fl oz double or
   whipping cream
250g/9oz strawberries

METHOD
1. Heat the oven to 120°C/250°F/ gas ½ and grease and line a baking sheet.
2. Beat the egg whites until stiff. Using a metal spoon, gradually add half the sugar a spoonful at a time, beating continuously, until the mixture holds soft peaks when you lift out the whisk. Using a large metal spoon, continue to fold in the remaining sugar and the vanilla.
2. Place spoonfuls of the meringue on the prepared baking sheet and shape the sides to make tiny baskets.

Alternatively, spoon the meringue into a piping bag with a large nozzle and pipe basket shapes on to the paper.
4. Bake in the oven for 1 hour until pale cream. Lift the meringues off the paper, turn them upside down and return to the oven for a further 20 minutes until completely dry.
5. Whip the cream until stiff. Spoon into the meringue baskets, then fill with the strawberries.

CHAPTER 10

* * * * * * * *

ICINGS & FILLINGS

A layer of icing can liven up a plain cake, make a birthday or celebration cake extra special — or even disguise a cake that is not as good-looking as it might be! Here is a selection of icings, frostings and fillings suitable to mix and match with all your favourite cakes.

The icing on the cake

✳ ✳ ✳ ✳ ✳ ✳ ✳ ✳

Some cakes don't need any additions; others are crying out for a little decoration. But don't go overboard with icings and swamp the flavour of the cake.

When you are choosing whether or not to ice a cake, think first about how it looks. If it has a beautiful, sugar-coated top or a lovely golden crust, then the last thing you want to do is hide it. But for children's cakes the other extreme is usually what is wanted. Go for colour, variety and exuberance, and make a show!

In between, you are looking for contrast and complement. A contrasting colour can look stunning, and offering a sharp flavour against a rich one will work well – such as a lemon icing on a treacle gingerbread.

Make sure your flavours don't fight with each other. Particular flavours and textures are commonly put together because they set each other off so well, so if you are not sure, go for the traditional pairings before you experiment.

When you are mixing liquid into icing sugar, you might think it is never going to absorb the water and create a smooth icing. Don't be tempted to pour in lots more water – be patient and continue to add it just a drop at a time as you mix. It needs quite a lot of time, but only a little water.

OTHER ICINGS
You will find other icings under individual recipes:
Caramel buttercream (page 64)
Cream cheese frosting with cloves (page102)
Cream cheese frosting with honey and lemon (page 103)
Cream cheese icing with nutmeg (page 104)
Devil's food cake frosting (page 80)
Honey frosting (page 50)
Toffee icing (page 108)

Glacé Icing

✳ ✳ ✳ ✳ ✳ ✳ ✳ ✳

Glacé icing is easy to make and can be created with all kinds of variations, so you can choose your colour or flavour to suit any type of cake.

INGREDIENTS *Makes enough to cover a 20cm/8in cake*
100g/4oz icing sugar, sifted
1 tbsp hot water

METHOD

1. Sift the icing sugar into a small bowl.
2. Add the water a few drops at a time, stirring with a wooden spoon until you have a smooth icing; you may not need all the water. Do not add it too quickly or the icing will be too runny. If this happens, simply add some more icing sugar.
3. Spoon over the cake and leave to set.

VARIATIONS

Almond glacé icing Add a few drops of almond extract before you start to add the water.

Chocolate glacé icing Use 75g/3oz icing sugar and 25g/1oz cocoa powder instead of all icing sugar.
Coloured glacé icing Add a few drops of your chosen food colour with the water and remember that you will need less water.
Lemon glacé icing Add the grated zest of ½ lemon and a few drops of lemon juice and use slightly less water.
Mocha glacé icing Use 75g/3oz icing sugar, 2 tbsp of cocoa powder and 2 tbsp instant coffee granules, crushed, instead of just icing sugar.
Orange glacé icing Add the grated zest of ¼ orange and a few drops of orange juice before you start to add the water.
Vanilla glacé icing Add a few drops of vanilla extract before you start to add the water.

Buttercream

Make sure you start with softened butter for your icing to make it easier to work. Leave it at room temperature for an hour before you use it, or use a suitable spread.

INGREDIENTS *Makes enough to cover or fill a 20cm/8in cake*

100g/4oz butter, softened
275g/10oz icing sugar, sifted
1 tbsp milk

METHOD

1. Beat the butter in a bowl until soft.
2. Gradually beat in the icing sugar and milk until the icing is smooth and soft.
3. Spread over the cake and chill before serving.

VARIATIONS

Chocolate buttercream Use 250g/9oz icing sugar and 50g/2oz cocoa powder instead of just icing sugar.
Coffee buttercream Dissolve 2 tsp of instant coffee in 1 tbsp hot water, then leave to cool and use instead of the milk.
Coloured buttercream Add a few drops of food colouring of your choice instead of some of the milk.
Honey buttercream Replace the milk with 1 tbsp strongly flavoured honey.
Lemon buttercream Replace the milk with 1 tbsp lemon juice and add ½ tsp finely grated lemon zest.
Mocha buttercream Use 75g/3oz cocoa powder and only 200g/7oz icing sugar. Dissolve 2 tsp of instant coffee in 1 tbsp hot water, then leave to cool and use in place of the milk.
Orange buttercream Replace the milk with 1 tbsp orange juice and add a little finely grated orange zest.
Vanilla buttercream Add a few drops of vanilla extract to the basic mix.

American Frosting

This is a light frosting that you can use on almost any cake. It is very simple to make and you can flavour it in a variety of ways, from vanilla to chocolate.

INGREDIENTS *Makes enough to cover a 20cm/8in cake*

40g/1½oz butter
25g/1oz golden syrup
2 tbsp milk
175g/6oz icing sugar, sifted
2 tsp vanilla extract

METHOD

1. Melt the butter, syrup and milk in a pan over a low heat, then bring just to the boil. Remove from the heat.

2. Put the icing sugar in a bowl. Pour in the hot mixture and add the vanilla. Stir with a wooden spoon until smooth.

3. To ice a cake, spoon the icing over while warm.

4. To use as a filling or frosting, leave to cool, then beat until thick and creamy.

VARIATIONS

Chocolate frosting Add 50g/2oz dark chocolate to the melted mixture.

Coffee frosting Replace the vanilla extract with 2 tsp cooled strong black coffee.

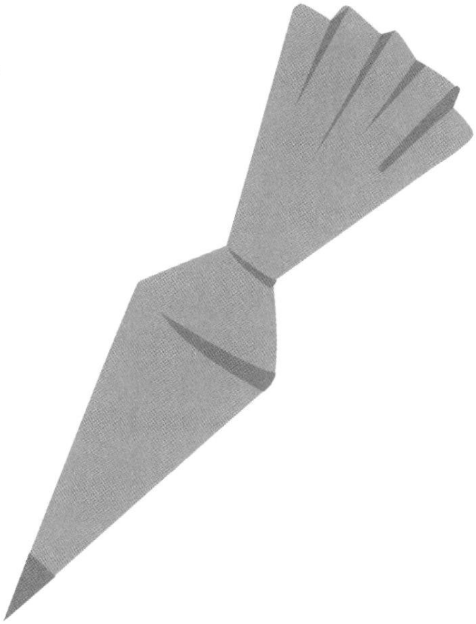

Rich Chocolate Icing

✳ ✳ ✳ ✳ ✳ ✳ ✳ ✳

*Since this is a very rich icing, use it sparingly on plain cakes,
either as a filling between layers or spread over the top of the cake.*

INGREDIENTS *Makes enough to
cover a 20cm/8in cake*
100g/4oz dark chocolate
1 tbsp water
50g/2oz butter
100g/4oz icing sugar, sifted
1 egg yolk

METHOD
1. Melt the chocolate and water in
a heatproof bowl set over a pan of
gently simmering water.
2. Beat together the butter and sugar
until pale and creamy. Beat in the egg
yolk, then beat in the chocolate.
3. Spread over the cake and leave
to set.

EGG WHITES TO SPARE
You need never waste
egg whites when
you have used only
the yolks in a recipe.
Add the whites
to omelettes and
flans, use them in
cakes, or make some
meringues (page
146–148).

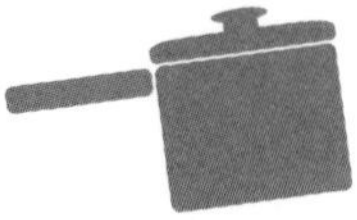

Fondant Icing

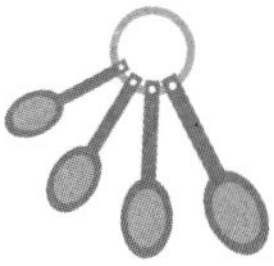

You can buy fondant icing ready-made in the supermarket, but it is very satisfying to make your own. It dries out quickly, so keep it well wrapped when you are not using it.

INGREDIENTS *Makes enough to cover a 20cm/8in cake*

150ml/5fl oz water
450g/1lb caster sugar
a pinch of cream of tartar
2 tsp water

METHOD

1. Put the water and sugar in a heavy-based pan over a low heat and leave until the sugar has dissolved. If there are any sugar crystals stuck to the sides of the pan, dip a pastry brush in cold water to wipe the sugar into the syrup.

2. Dissolve the cream of tartar in the water and add it to the pan. Increase the heat and boil until the syrup reaches 116°C/240°F. A drop of the syrup will form a soft ball when dropped into cold water.

3. Slowly pour the syrup into a heat-resistant bowl and leave until a skin forms on the top. Stir in a figure of eight movement until it turns opaque and becomes thick, then knead it until smooth. Wrap and keep in a airtight container until required.

4. When ready to use, place in a heatproof bowl over a pan of simmering water and warm, stirring in a little sugar syrup until the icing looks like thick cream, then spread over the cake.

SUGAR THERMOMETER

If you are going to do a lot of baking, a sugar thermometer is very useful. If you are making icing, caramel or other sugar syrups, the temperature is crucial to how the sugar behaves.

Royal Icing

✳ ✳ ✳ ✳ ✳ ✳ ✳ ✳

You will need a little time to leave this to rest, so make sure you plan ahead so that you can get the best results.

INGREDIENTS *Makes enough to cover a 25cm/10in cake*
4 egg whites
900g/2lb icing sugar, sifted
1 tbsp lemon juice
2 tsp glycerine

METHOD
1. Whisk the egg whites in a large bowl until frothy.
2. Gradually beat in half the icing sugar, then the lemon juice. Continue to beat in the icing sugar until the mixture forms soft peaks when you pull out the whisk. You may not need all the sugar. If you are piping the icing, make it a little stiffer. Stir in the glycerine.
3. Wrap in clingfilm and leave to rest in the fridge for 24 hours, if possible.
4. Beat lightly before spreading on the cake.

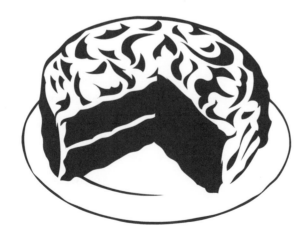

Almond Paste

❋ ❋ ❋ ❋ ❋ ❋ ❋ ❋

Homemade almond paste is simple to make and will finish off your Christmas or simnel cake perfectly with its intense almond flavour.

INGREDIENTS *Makes enough to cover a 23cm/9in cake*
225g/8oz caster sugar
225g/8oz icing sugar, sifted
450g/1lb ground almonds
2 eggs
2 egg yolks
2 tsp lemon juice
a few drops of vanilla extract

METHOD
1. In a bowl, mix together the sugars and ground almonds.
2. In a separate bowl, mix together the eggs, egg yolks, lemon juice and vanilla.
3. Combine the two and beat until they start to come together, then use your hands to knead gently into a smooth ball. Do not overbeat or the paste will be greasy.
4. Wrap in clingfilm and chill until ready to roll out.

PETIT FOURS

With hands dusted in icing sugar, shape tiny pieces of almond paste into balls and place in paper sweet cases. Decorate with flaked almonds, sliced dates, glacé cherries or dried fruit.

Index

�֎ �֎ ✣ ✣ ✣ ✣ ✣ ✣